RUSSIA:
FROM WORKERS' STATE
TO STATE CAPITALISM

The International Socialism book series (IS Books) aims to make available books that explain the theory and historical practice of working class self-emancipation from below. In so doing, we hope to rescue the main tenets of the revolutionary socialist tradition from its detractors on both the right and left. This is an urgent challenge for the left today, as we seek to rebuild this tradition in circumstances that often downplay the importance of organized revolutionaries.

By reissuing classics of the international socialist tradition, we hope to offer accessible and unique resources for today's generation of socialists.

Other titles in the International Socialism series:

Leon Trotsky and the Organizational Principles of the Revolutionary Party
Dianne Feeley, Paul Le Blanc, and Thomas Twiss,
introduction by George Breitman

Mandate of Heaven: Marx and Mao in Modern China
Nigel Harris

The Duncan Hallas Reader (forthcoming)
Edited by Ahmed Shawki

The Lost Revolution: Germany 1918 to 1923
Chris Harman

Marxism and the Party
John Molyneux

Party and Class
Tony Cliff, Duncan Hallas, Chris Harman, and Leon Trotsky

Russia: From Workers' State to State Capitalism
Anthony Arnove, Tony Cliff, Chris Harman, and Ahmed Shawki

RUSSIA:
FROM WORKERS' STATE
TO STATE CAPITALISM

ANTHONY ARNOVE

PETER BINNS

TONY CLIFF

CHRIS HARMAN

AHMED SHAWKI

Haymarket Books
Chicago, Illinois

The first four chapters of this book were originally published in 1987 by Bookmarks (London and Chicago).

"80 years since the Russian Revolution" by Ahmed Shawki first appeared in the *International Socialist Review*, issue 3, Winter 1997.

"The fall of Stalinism: Ten years on" by Anthony Arnove first appeared in the *International Socialist Review*, issue 10, Winter 2000.

This edition published in 2003 and 2017 by
Haymarket Books
P.O. Box 180165
Chicago, IL 60618
773-583-7884
www.haymarketbooks.org
info@haymarketbooks.org

ISBN: 978-1-60846-545-3

Trade distribution:
In the US, Consortium Book Sales and Distribution, www.cbsd.com
In Canada, Publishers Group Canada, www.pgcbooks.ca
In the UK, Turnaround Publisher Services, www.turnaround-uk.com
All other countries, Ingram Publisher Services International,
intlsales@perseusbooks.com

This book was published with the generous support of Lannan Foundation and Wallace Action Fund.

Cover design by Eric Kerl.

Printed in Canada by union labor.

Library of Congress Cataloging-in-Publication data is available.

10 9 8 7 6 5 4 3 2 1

Contents

ONE

WORKERS' REVOLUTION AND BEYOND

TONY CLIFF

ONLY TWICE IN HISTORY has the working class taken state power: in the Paris Commune of 1871 and the Russian Revolution of 1917. The Paris Commune demonstrated the heroism of the working class, its capacity to seize state power and to start, however haltingly, to reshape society.

But the industrial working class of Paris was tiny, employed mainly in small workshops, without a party to lead it, and without a clear theory to guide it. The Russian Revolution brought to power a much more mature, better organised and politically conscious working class. Never before had the working class become the ruling class of a great country, fighting tenaciously and heroically against class enemies at home and against invading foreign armies. Never before had such radical changes in social structure been carried out in so short a time. Semi-feudal social relations of land ownership were swept away far more radically than even in the French Revolution of 1789. Practically all the factories, mines and other valuable natural resources of the country were taken over by the workers' state.

A number of decrees of world historical importance were issued by the newly established workers' government: the decree on land, which transferred the property of the landlords to the millions of peasants; the decree on workers' control over production, which made the workers the masters in the factories; the decree on self-determination, which gave full freedom to the oppressed nations of Russia; the decrees that swept

1

away the old marriage and divorce laws. According to these decrees only civil marriage was to be recognised by the state; children born out of wedlock were to be given the same rights as those born in marriage; divorce was to be had for the asking by either spouse. The new laws emphasised the full equality of men and women. Adultery and homosexuality were dropped from the criminal code.

The Russian working class faced extreme obstacles on its way. The French Revolution of 1789 had taken place in a country that at the time had achieved the highest level of economic and cultural development in the world, with the possible exception of England. Russia in 1917 was one of the most backward countries in Europe. And from the outset the Russian bourgeoisie resorted to harsh counter-revolutionary measures, calling on the support of world capitalism. The Russian White armies were aided by no fewer than fourteen foreign expeditionary forces, including those of Britain, France, the United States, Japan, Germany, Italy and Turkey.

Russia emerged from the civil war in a state of economic collapse 'unparalleled in the history of mankind', as one economic historian of the period put it. Industrial production was about one fifth of the level it had been before the outbreak of the First World War in 1914. The population of the cities had shrunk. The most revolutionary workers had joined the Red Army in defence of the revolution. Others, driven by lack of food and fuel, had returned to the peasant villages. Between the end of 1918 and the end of 1920 epidemics, hunger and cold had killed nine million Russians (the war as a whole had claimed four million victims).

From the first day Lenin and Trotsky had made it clear that the survival of workers' power in Russia would depend on the victory of revolution elsewhere in the world. The Russian revolution was only the beginning of the world socialist revolution. Lenin told the Third Congress of Soviets on 11 January 1918: 'The final victory of socialism in a single country is of course impossible. Our contingent of workers and peasants which is upholding Soviet power is one of the contingents of the great world army.'[1] 'It is the absolute truth that without a German revolution we are doomed,' he said a short while later.[2]

The October revolution in Russia did find an echo elsewhere—with revolutions in Germany, Austria and Hungary spreading revolutionary waves throughout Europe. The tiny Communist groups of 1919 grew into mass working-class parties. For a while the future hung in the balance.

But the leaderships of these new Communist Parties were young and inexperienced, and unable to overcome the counter-revolutionary activities of the old-established social-democratic parties. The revolutions in Europe were defeated. Russia remained isolated.

The question that socialists who look back to the hope and inspiration offered by the revolution of 1917 have to answer is this: how was it that this revolution, which came closer to working-class self-emancipation than ever before, was followed by the rise of the ruling bureaucracy headed by Stalin? It was to answer this question that Chris Harman wrote his article 'Russia: How the revolution was lost', first published in 1968 and reprinted below.

After the end of the Second World War, further regimes were set up on the Stalinist model, first in Eastern Europe, then in China. The second article reprinted below, Chris Harman's 'The Nature of Stalinist Russia and the Eastern Bloc', was first published in 1971. The appearance of these regimes challenged Trotsky's perception of the Stalinist regime as a 'degenerated workers' state'. For their establishment involved no workers' revolution; in Eastern Europe the Russian army was used to ensure that Communists obedient to Moscow were able to gain control over the state apparatus; in China Mao Tse-tung marched to victory at the head of an overwhelmingly peasant army. As I wrote in 1950:

> If state property, planning and the monopoly of foreign trade define a country as a workers' state, then without doubt Russia as well as the 'new democracies' [of Eastern Europe] are workers' states. This means that in the latter proletarian revolutions have taken place. These were led by the Stalinists on the basis of national unity, governmental coalitions with the bourgeoisie and chauvinism which led to the expulsion of millions of German toilers and their families. Such policies merely served to oil the wheels of the proletarian revolution . . .
>
> If the social revolution took place in the Eastern European countries without a revolutionary proletarian leadership, we must conclude that in future social revolutions, as in past ones, the masses will do the fighting but not the leading. To assume that the 'new democracies' are workers' states means to accept that in principle the proletarian revolution is, just as the bourgeois wars were, based on the deception of the people.
>
> If the 'new democracies' are workers' states, Stalin has realised the proletarian revolution . . . If these countries are workers' states, then why Marxism, why the Fourth International?

If the 'new democracies' are workers' states, what Marx and Engels said about the socialist revolution being 'history conscious of itself' is refuted. Refuted is Engels' statement: 'It is only from this point [the socialist revolution] that men, with full consciousness, will fashion their own history; it is only from this point that the social causes set in motion by men will have, predominantly and in constantly increasing measure, the effects willed by men. It is humanity's leap from the realm of necessity into the realm of freedom.'

Rosa Luxemburg, too, must have spoken nonsense in her summing-up of what all the Marxist teachers wrote about the place of proletarian consciousness in a revolution: 'In all the class struggles of the past . . . one of the essential conditions of action was the ignorance of [the] masses with regard to the real aims of the struggle, its material content, and its limits. This discrepancy was, in fact, the specific historical basis of the "leading role" of the "enlightened" bourgeoisie, which corresponded with the role of the masses as docile followers . . . That is why the enlightenment of the masses with regard to their tasks and methods is an indispensible historical condition for socialist action, just as in former periods the ignorance of the masses was the condition for the action of the dominant classes.'[3]

The third article reprinted below is Peter Binns' 'The Theory of State Capitalism', first published in 1975. After the October revolution, humanity stood at the crossroads. There were two clear choices: the revolution could have spread internationally, leading to the victory of socialism throughout the world, or the counter-revolution could have smashed the young Soviet Republic. In the event, neither happened. The revolutions in Germany, Austria and Hungary were defeated—but at the same time the forces of world capitalism failed to defeat the Russian Soviet Republic. An uneasy equilibrium was reached. An inevitable result of this was the transformation of the economic, social and political order in Russia.

All struggles impose a symmetry upon the antagonists. If a vicious dog attacks me, I have no alternative but to act symmetrically. This does not mean I have to bite the dog. After all, my teeth are not up to that. But I shall have to use violence—say, a stick—in answer to its violence. If the vicious dog kills me, the symmetry will be at an end, and if I kill the dog, likewise. But if I was not strong enough to kill the dog and it was not strong enough to kill me, and for months we co-exist fighting one another, the symmetry will continue—until any onlooker could not make up his or her mind which of us was the cause of the viciousness.

Russia was forced to build a massive military-industrial machine in answer to the military and industrial might of world imperialism. Competition between capitalists, whether individuals or states, forces each to accumulate, accumulate, accumulate. As Marx put it: 'Accumulation for accumulation's sake, production for production's sake: by this formula classical economy expressed the historical mission of the bourgeoisie, and did not for a single instant deceive itself over the birth-throes of wealth.'[4]

In Russia the horrors of forced industrialisation, of the brutal collectivisation of the peasantry, the deprivation of workers of their rights to organise in trade unions or to strike, the police terror, all were the by-products of an unprecedented rate of capital accumulation. In Britain the industrial revolution spanned a century and involved a population of some eight to fifteen million; it had the supporting benefit of the slave trade and the robbery of colonies around the world. In Russia the industrial revolution under Stalin spanned one generation and involved between 160 and 200 million people. The horrors of the industrial revolution in Britain were reproduced on a far larger scale in Russia.

The symmetry between world capitalism and the Stalinist regime has come about not in one, but in two ways. The pressures of world capitalism brought about the state capitalist order in Russia—but cause and effect may change places, and the state capitalist regime in Russia in its turn helped to create the permanent arms economy that has dominated world capitalism over the past half-century.

Our analysis of the class nature of Russia under Stalin, and today, differs from that made by Leon Trotsky. But the roots of our analysis are in Trotsky's general ideas: his internationalism, his opposition to the theory of 'socialism in one country', his hatred of the Stalinist bureaucracy, his revolutionary confidence in the initiative and power of the working class—these are our inspiration. When one stands on the shoulders of a giant, one can, with good eyesight, see very far indeed.

TWO

HOW THE REVOLUTION
WAS LOST

CHRIS HARMAN

THE REVOLUTION OF 1917 gave control of a major country to a workers' government for the first time in history. To millions throughout a world locked in a savage and futile war, it offered new hope. In the period afterwards people everywhere turned from the grim alternatives of a declining capitalism—unemployment, poverty, fascist barbarity, the threat of new wars—to place their hopes for the future in the regime that the Soviets (councils of ordinary working men and women) had put into power in Russia.

Yet today the government of the USSR inspires support from few on the left. Its brutal suppression of the Hungarian revolution in 1956 turned thousands of militants against it. When it repeated, albeit in a less bloody form, such an act of aggression against a 'socialist' country in Czechoslovakia, even the official Communist Parties turned against it in a half-hearted fashion. Meanwhile its posturings vis-à-vis China—from withdrawing much needed technical aid to threatening full-scale war over a few barren border areas—have disillusioned those who even today manage to praise Stalin.

What did happen in the fateful years after the revolution? What went wrong? Who was to blame?

First published in *International Socialism*, first series, number 30, in 1967. Reprinted as a pamphlet 1969.

The two revolutions

The period between the two revolutions of February and October 1917 was moulded by two concurrent processes. The first occurred in the towns, and was a very rapid growth of working-class consciousness. By the July days, the industrial workers at least seem to have arrived at an understanding of the different interests of the classes in the revolution. In the countryside, a different form of class differentiation took place. This was not, as in the cities, between a propertied class—the bourgeoisie— and a class that could not even aspire to individual ownership of property—the workers. Rather it was between two property-owning classes: on the one hand the landowners, on the other the peasants. The latter were not socialist in intention. Their aim was to seize the estates of the landowners, but to divide these up on an individualistic basis. In this movement even *kulaks*, wealthy farmers, could participate.

The revolution could not have taken place without the simultane- ous occurrence of these two processes. What tied them together was not however an identity of ultimate aim. Rather it was the fact that for contingent historical reasons the industrial bourgeoisie could not break politically with the large landowners. Its inability to do this pushed the peasantry (which effectively included the army) and the workers into the same camp:

> In order to realise the soviet state, there was required the drawing together and mutual penetration of two factors belonging to completely differ- ent historic species: a peasant war—that is a movement characteristic of the dawn of bourgeois development—and a proletarian insurrection, the movement signalising its decline.[1]

The urban insurrection could not have succeeded but for the sym- pathy of the largely peasant army. Nor could the peasants have waged a successful struggle unless led and welded together by a centralised, external force. In Russia of 1917 the only possible such force was the organised working class. It was this ability to draw the peasantry behind it at the crucial moment that made it possible for the workers to hold power in the towns.

The bourgeoisie and its land-owning allies were expropriated. But the classes which participated in this expropriation shared no simple long-term common interest. In the towns was a class whose very exist- ence depended upon collective activity; in the countryside a class whose members would only unite even amongst themselves momentarily to seize the land, but would then till it individually. Once the act of seizure and defence of that seizure was over, only external inducements could bind them to any state.

The revolution, then, was really a dictatorship of the workers over other classes in the towns—in the major towns the rule of the majority in *soviets* or workers' councils—and a dictatorship of the towns over the country. In the first period of the division of the estates this dictatorship could rely upon peasant support, indeed, was defended by peasant bayonets. But what was to happen afterwards?

This question had preoccupied the Russian socialists themselves long before the revolution. The realisation that a socialist revolution in Russia would be hopelessly lost in the peasant mass was one reason why all the Marxists in Russia (including Lenin, but excluding Trotsky and at first Parvus) had seen the forthcoming revolution as a bourgeois one. When Parvus and Trotsky first suggested that the revolution might produce a socialist government, Lenin wrote:

> This cannot be, because such a revolutionary dictatorship can only have stability . . . based on the great majority of the people. The Russian proletariat constitutes now a minority of the Russian population.

He maintained this view right up to 1917. When he did come to accept and fight for the possibility of a socialist outcome for the revolution, it was because he saw it as one stage in a worldwide revolution that would give the minority working class in Russia protection against foreign intervention and aid to reconcile the peasantry to its rule. Eight months before the October revolution he wrote to Swiss workers that 'the Russian proletariat cannot by its own forces victoriously complete the socialist revolution.' Four months after the revolution (on 7 March 1918) he repeated: 'The absolute truth is that without a revolution in Germany we shall perish.'

The civil war

The first years of soviet rule–seemed to bear out the perspective of world revolution. The period 1918-19 was characterised by social upheavals unseen since 1848. In Germany and Austria military defeat was followed by the destruction of the monarchy. Everywhere there was talk of soviets. In Hungary and Bavaria soviet governments actually took power—although only briefly. In Italy the factories were occupied. Yet the heritage of fifty years of gradual development was not to be erased so rapidly. The old Social-Democratic and trade-union leaders moved into the gap left by the discredited bourgeois parties. The Communist left on the other hand still lacked the organisation to respond to this. It acted when there was no mass support; when there was mass support it failed to act.

Even so the stabilisation of Europe after 1919 was at best precarious. In every European country, the social structure received severe threats within the subsequent fifteen years. And the experience of both the Communist Parties and the working class had put them into a far better position to understand what was happening.

The Russian Bolsheviks did not, however, intend to wait upon the revolution abroad. The defence of the soviet republic and incitement to revolution abroad seemed inseparable. For the time being anyway, the tasks at hand in Russia were determined, not by the Bolshevik leaders, but by the international imperialist powers. These had begun a 'crusade' against the soviet republic. The counter-revolutionary 'white' and foreign armies had to be driven back before any other questions could be considered. In order to do this, every resource available had to be utilised.

By a mixture of popular support, revolutionary ardour, and, at times, it seemed, pure will, the counter-revolutionary forces were driven out (although in the far east of Russia they continued to operate until 1924). But the price paid was enormous.

This cannot be counted in merely material terms. But in these terms alone it was great. What suffered above all was industrial and agricultural production. In 1920 the production of pig iron was only 3 per cent of the pre-war figure, of hemp 10 per cent, flax 25 per cent, cotton 11 per cent, beets 15 per cent. This implied privation, hardship, famine. But much more. The dislocation of industrial production was also the dislocation of the working class, which was reduced to 43 per cent of its former numbers. The others had returned to their villages or were dead on the battlefield. In purely quantitative terms, the class that had led the revolution, the class whose democratic processes had constituted the living core of soviet power, was halved in importance.

In real terms the situation was even worse. What remained was not even half of that class, forced into collective action by the very nature of its life situation. Industrial output was only 18 per cent of the pre-war figure; labour productivity was only one-third of what it had been. To keep alive, workers could not rely on what their collective product would buy. Many resorted to direct barter of their products—or even parts of their machines—with peasants in return for food. Not only was the leading class of the revolution decimated, but the ties linking its members together were fast disintegrating.

The very personnel in the factories were not those who had constituted the core of the revolutionary movement of 1917. The most militant workers had quite naturally fought most at the front during the civil war, and suffered most casualties. Those that survived were needed not only in the factories, but as cadres in the army, or as commissars to keep the administrators operating the state machine. Raw peasants from the countryside, without socialist traditions or aspirations, took their place.

But what was to be the fate of the revolution if the class that made it ceased to exist in any meaningful sense? This was not a problem that the Bolshevik leaders could have foreseen. They had always said that isolation of the revolution would result in its destruction by foreign armies and domestic counter-revolution. What confronted them now was the success of counter-revolution from abroad in destroying the class that had led the revolution while leaving intact the state apparatus built up by it. The revolutionary power had survived; but radical changes were being produced in its internal composition.

From soviet power to Bolshevik dictatorship

The revolutionary institutions of 1917—above all the soviets—were organically connected with the class that had led the revolution. Between the aspirations and intentions of their members and those of the workers who had elected them, there could be no gap. While the mass supported the Menshevik Party, the soviets were Menshevik; when the mass began to follow the Bolsheviks, so did the soviets. The Bolshevik Party was merely the body of coordinated class-conscious militants who could frame policies and suggest courses of action alongside other such bodies, in the soviets as in the factories themselves. Their coherent views and self-discipline meant that they could act to implement policies effectively—but only if the mass of workers would follow them.

Even consistent opponents of the Bolsheviks recognised this. Their leading Menshevik critic wrote:

> Understand, please, that before us after all is a victorious uprising of the proletariat—almost the entire proletariat supports Lenin and expects its social liberation from the uprising . . . [2]

Until the civil war was well under way, this democratic dialectic of party and class could continue. The Bolsheviks held power as the majority party in the soviets. But other parties continued to exist there too. The Mensheviks continued to operate legally and compete with the Bolsheviks for support until June 1918.

The decimation of the working class changed all this. Of necessity the soviet institutions took on a life independently of the class they had arisen from. Those workers and peasants who fought the civil war could not govern themselves collectively from their places in the factories. The socialist workers spread over the length and breadth of the war zones had to be organised and coordinated by a centralised governmental apparatus independent of their direct control—at least temporarily.

It seemed to the Bolsheviks that such a structure could not be held together unless it contained within it only those who wholeheartedly supported the revolution—that is, only the Bolsheviks. The Right Social Revolutionaries were instigators of the counter-revolution. The Left Social Revolutionaries were willing to resort to terror when they disagreed with government policy. As for the Mensheviks, their policy was one of support for the Bolsheviks against the counter-revolution, with the demand that they hand over power to the Constituent Assembly (one of the chief demands of the counter-revolution). In practice this meant that the Menshevik Party contained both supporters and opponents of the soviet power. Many of its members went over to the side of the Whites (for example Menshevik organisations in the Volga area were sympathetic to the counter-revolutionary Samara government, and one member of the Menshevik central committee, Ivan Maisky—later Stalin's ambassador—joined it).[3] The response of the Bolsheviks was to allow the party's members their freedom (at least, most of the time), but to prevent them acting as an effective political force—for example they were allowed no press after June 1918 except for three months in the following year.

In all this the Bolsheviks had no choice. They could not give up power just because the class they represented had dissolved itself while fighting to defend that power. Nor could they tolerate the propagation of ideas that undermined the basis of its power—precisely because the working class itself no longer existed as an agency collectively organised so as to be able to determine its own interests.

Of necessity the soviet state of 1917 had been replaced by the single-party state of 1920 onwards. The soviets that remained were increasingly just a front for Bolshevik power (although other parties, such as the Mensheviks, continued to operate in them as late as 1920). By 1919, for instance, there were no elections to the Moscow Soviet for over 18 months.[4]

Kronstadt and the New Economic Policy

Paradoxically, the end of the civil war did not alleviate this situation, but in many ways aggravated it. For with the end of the immediate threat of counter-revolution, the cord that had bound together the two revolutionary processes—workers' power in the towns and peasant uprisings in the country—was cut. Having gained control over the land, the peasants lost interest in the collectivist revolutionary ideals of October. They were motivated by individual aspirations arising out of their individualistic form of work. Each sought to maximise his own standard of living through his activities on his own plot of land. Indeed, the only thing which could now unite peasants into a coherent group was opposition to the taxes and forcible collections of grain carried out in order to feed the urban populations.

The high point of this opposition came a week before the tenth Communist Party Congress in March 1921. An uprising of sailors broke out in the Kronstadt fortress, which guarded the approaches to Petrograd. Many people since have treated what happened next as the first break between the Bolshevik regime and its socialist intentions. The fact that the Kronstadt sailors were one of the main drives of the 1917 revolution has often been used as an argument for this. Yet at the time no one in the Bolshevik Party—not even the workers' opposition which claimed to represent the antipathy of many workers to the regime—had any doubts as to what it was necessary to do. The reason was simple. Kronstadt in 1920 was not Kronstadt of 1917. The class composition of its sailors had changed. The best socialist elements had long ago gone off to fight in the army in the front line. They were replaced in the main by peasants whose devotion to the revolution was that of their class. This was reflected in the demands of the uprising: soviets without Bolsheviks and a free market in agriculture.

The Bolshevik leaders could not accede to such demands. It would have meant liquidation of the socialist aims of the revolution without struggle. For all its faults, it was precisely the Bolshevik Party that had alone wholeheartedly supported soviet power, while the other parties, even the socialist parties, had vacillated between it and the Whites. It was to the Bolsheviks that all the best militants had been attached. Soviets without Bolsheviks could only mean soviets without the party which had consistently sought to express the socialist, collectivist aims of the working class in the revolution.

What was expressed in Kronstadt was the fundamental divergence of interest, in the long run, between the two classes that had made the revolution. The suppression of the uprising should be seen not as an attack on the socialist content of the revolution, but as a desperate attempt, using force, to prevent the developing peasant opposition to its collectivist ends from destroying it.[5]

Yet the fact that Kronstadt could occur was an omen. For it questioned the whole leading role of the working class in the revolution. This was being maintained not by the superior economic mode that the working class represented, not by its higher labour productivity and collectivity, but by physical force. And this force was not being wielded directly by the armed workers, but by a party tied to the working class only indirectly, by its ideas, not directly as in the days of 1917.

Such a policy was necessary. But there was little in it that socialists could have supported in any other situation. Instead of being 'the self-conscious, independent movement of the immense majority in the interest of the immense majority', the revolution in Russia had reached the stage where it involved the exploitation of the country by the towns, maintained through naked physical force. It was clear to all groups in the Bolshevik Party that this meant the revolution must remain in danger of being overthrown by peasant insurrections.

There seemed to be only one course open. This was to accept many of the peasant demands, while maintaining a strong, centralised socialist state apparatus. This the New Economic Policy (NEP) attempted to do. Its aim was to reconcile peasants to the regime and to encourage economic development by giving a limited range of freedom to private commodity production. The state and the state-owned industries were to operate as just one element in an economy governed by the needs of peasant production and the play of market forces.

The party, the state and the working class 1921–28

In the period of the NEP the claim of Russia to be in any way 'socialist' could no longer be justified either by the relationship of the working class to the state it had orginally created or by the nature of internal economic relations. The workers did not exercise power and the economy was not planned. But the state, the 'body of armed men' that controlled and policed society, was in the hands of a party that was motivated by socialist intentions. The direction of its policies, it seemed, would be socialist.

Yet the situation was more complex than this. First, the state institutions that dominated Russian society were far from identical with the militant socialist party of 1917. Those who had been in the Bolshevik Party at the time of the February revolution were committed socialists who had taken enormous risks in resisting Tsarist oppression to express their ideals. Even four years of civil war and isolation from the working masses could not easily destroy their socialist aspirations. But in 1919 these constituted only a tenth of the party, by 1922 a fortieth.

In the revolution and civil war, the party had undergone a continuous process of growth. In part this reflected the tendency of all militant workers and convinced socialists to join in. But it was also a result of other tendencies. Once the working class itself had been decimated, the party had had to take it upon itself to control all soviet-run areas. This it could only do by increasing its own size. Further, once it was clear who was winning the civil war, many individuals with little or no socialist convictions attempted to enter the party. The party itself was thus far from being a homogeneous socialist force. At best, only its leading elements and most militant members could be said to be really part of the socialist tradition.

This internal dilution of the party was paralleled by a corresponding phenomenon in the state apparatus itself. In order to maintain control over Russian society, the Bolshevik Party had been forced to use thousands of members of the old Tsarist bureaucracy in order to maintain a functioning governmental machine. In theory the Bolsheviks were to direct the work of these in a socialist direction. In practice, old habits and methods of work, prerevolutionary attitudes towards the masses in particular, often prevailed. Lenin was acutely aware of the implications of this; he told the March 1922 party congress:

> What we lack is clear enough. The ruling stratum of the communists is lacking in culture. Let us look at Moscow. This mass of bureaucrats—who

is leading whom? The 4,700 responsible communists, the mass of burea-
crats, or the other way round? I do not believe you can honestly say the
communists are leading this mass. To put it honestly, they are not the
leaders but the led.

At the end of 1922, he described the state apparatus as 'borrowed
from Tsarism and hardly touched by the soviet world . . . a bourgeois and
Tsarist mechanism.'[6] In the 1920 controversy over the role of the trade
unions he argued:

Ours is not actually a workers' state, but a workers' and peasants' state . . .
But that is not all. Our party programme shows that ours is a workers'
state with bureaucratic distortions.[7]

The real situation was even worse than this. It was not just the case
that the old Bolsheviks were in a situation where the combined strength
of hostile class forces and bureaucratic inertness made their socialist
aspirations difficult to realise. These aspirations themselves could not
remain forever uncorrupted by the hostile environment. The exigencies
of building a disciplined army out of an often indifferent peasant mass
had inculcated into many of the best party members authoritarian habits.

Under the NEP the situation was different, but still far from the
democratic interaction of leaders and led that constitutes the essence of
socialist democracy. Now many party members found themselves having
to control society by coming to terms with the small trader, the petty
capitalist, the *kulak*. They had to represent the interests of the workers'
state as against these elements—but not as in the past through direct
physical confrontation. There had to be limited co-operation with them.
Many party members seemed more influenced by this immediate and
very tangible relationship with petty bourgeois elements than by their
intangible ties with a weak and demoralised working class.

Above all, the influence of the old bureaucracy in which its members were immersed penetrated the party. Its isolation from class forces
outside itself that would sustain its rule meant that the party had to
exert over itself an iron discipline. Thus at the tenth party congress,
although it was presumed that discussion would continue within the
party,[8] the establishment of formal factions was 'temporarily' banned.
But this demand for inner cohesion easily degenerated into an accept-
ance of bureaucratic modes of control within the party. There had been

complaints about these by opposition elements in the party as early as April 1920. By 1922 even Lenin could write that 'we have a bureaucracy not only in the soviet institutions, but in the institutions of the party.'

The erosion of inner-party democracy is best shown by the fate of successive oppositions to the central leadership. In 1917 and 1918 free discussion within the party, with the right of different groups to organise around platforms, was taken for granted. Lenin himself was in a minority in the party on at least two occasions (at the time of his *April Theses* and nearly a year later during the Brest-Litovsk negotiations). In November 1917 it was possible for those Bolsheviks who disagreed with the party taking power alone, to resign from the government so as to force its hand, without disciplinary action being taken against then. Divisions within the party over the question of the advance of the Red Army on Warsaw and over the role of the trade unions were discussed quite openly in the party press. As late as 1921 the Programme of the Workers' Opposition was printed in a quarter of a million copies by the party itself, and two members of the opposition elected to the central committee. In 1923 when the Left Opposition developed, it was still possible for it to express its views in *Pravda*, although there were ten articles defending the leadership to every one opposing it.

Yet throughout this period the possibilities of any opposition acting effectively were diminished. After the tenth party congress the Workers' Opposition was banned. By 1923 the opposition 'Platform of the 46' wrote that 'the secretarial hierarchy of the party to an ever greater extent recruits the membership of conferences and congresses.'[9] Even a supporter of the leadership and editor of *Pravda*, Bukharin, depicted the typical functioning of the party as completely undemocratic:

> . . . the secretaries of the nuclei are usually appointed by the district committees, and note that the districts do not even try to have their candidates accepted by these nuclei, but content themselves with appointing these or those comrades. As a rule, putting the matter to a vote takes place according to a method that is taken for granted. The meeting is asked: 'Who is against?' and in as much as one fears more or less to speak up against, the appointed candidate finds himself elected . . . [10]

The real extent of bureaucratisation was fully revealed when the 'triumvirate', which had taken over the leadership of the party during the illness of Lenin, split. Lenin died in January 1924. Towards the end of

1925 Zinoviev, Kamenev and Krupskaya moved into opposition to the party centre, now controlled by Stalin. Zinoviev was head of the party in Leningrad. As such he controlled the administrative machine of the northern capital and several influential newspapers. At the fourteenth party congress every delegate from Leningrad supported his opposition to the centre. Yet within weeks of the defeat of his opposition, all sections of the party in Leningrad, with the exception of a few hundred inveterate oppositionists, were voting resolutions supporting Stalin's policies. All that was required to accomplish this was the removal from office of the heads of the city party administration. Who controlled the bureaucracy controlled the party. When Zinoviev controlled it, it was oppositional. Now that Stalin had added the city to the nation-wide apparatus he controlled, it became an adherent of his policies. With a change of leaders a Zinovievist monolith was transformed into a Stalinist monolith.

This rise of bureacracy in the soviet apparatus and the party began as a result of the decimation of the working class in the civil war. But it continued even when industry began to recover and the working class began to grow with the NEP. Economic recovery, rather than raising the position of the working class within the 'workers' state', depressed it.

In purely material terms the concessions made to the peasant in the NEP worsened the (relative) position of the worker.

> Everywhere acclaimed under war communism as the eponymous hero of the dictatorship of the proletariat, he was in danger of becoming the step-child of the NEP. In the economic crisis of 1923 neither the defenders of the official policy nor those who contested it in the name of the development of industry found it necessary to treat the grievances or the interests of the industrial worker as a matter of major concern.[11]

But it was not only vis-à-vis the peasant that the status of the worker fell; it also fell compared with that of the directors and managers of industry. Whereas in 1922, 65 per cent of managing personnel were officially classified as workers, and 35 per cent as non-workers, a year later these figures were almost reversed, only 36 per cent being workers and 64 per cent non-workers.[12] The 'red industrialists' began to emerge as a privileged group, with high salaries, and through 'one-man management' in the factories, able to hire and fire at will. At the same time widespread unemployment became endemic to the economy, rising to a level of one and a quarter million in 1923–24.

The divisions in the party 1921–29

Men make history, but in circumstances not of their own making. In the process they change both those circumstances and themselves. The Bolshevik Party was no more immune to this reality than any other group in history has been. In attempting to hold together the fabric of Russian society in the chaos of civil war, counter-revolution and famine, their socialist intentions were a factor determining the course of history; but the social forces they had to work with to do this could not leave the party members themselves unchanged.

Holding the Russia of the NEP together meant mediating between different social classes so as to prevent disruptive clashes. The revolution could only survive if the party and state satisfied the needs of different, often antagonistic, classes. Arrangements had to be made to satisfy the individualistic aspirations of the peasants, as well as the collectivist democratic aims of socialism. In the process, the party, which had been lifted above the different social classes, had to reflect their differences within its own structure. The pressures of the different classes on the party caused different sections of the party to define their socialist aspirations in terms of the interests of different classes. The one class with the capacity for exercising genuinely socialist pressures—the working class—was the weakest, the most disorganised, the least able to exert such pressures.

The Left Opposition

There can be no doubt that in terms of its ideas, the Left Opposition was the faction in the party that adhered most closely to the revolutionary socialist tradition of Bolshevism. It refused to redefine socialism to mean either a slowly developing peasant economy or accumulation for the sake of accumulation. It retained the view of workers' democracy as central to socialism. It refused to subordinate the world revolution to the demands of the chauvinistic and reactionary slogan of building 'socialism in one country'.

Yet the Left Opposition could not be said to be in any direct sense the 'proletarian' faction within the party. For in the Russia of the 1920s, the working class was the class that less than any other exerted pressure upon the party. After the civil war, it was rebuilt in conditions which made its ability to fight for its own ends weak. Unemployment was high; the most militant workers had either died in the civil war or been lifted into the bureaucracy; much of the class was composed of peasants fresh from the countryside. Its typical attitude was not one of support for the opposition, but rather apathy towards political discussions, which made it easily manipulable from above—at least most of the time. The Left Opposition was in the situation, common to socialists, of having a socialist programme for working-class action when the workers themselves were too tired and dispirited to fight.

But it was not only the apathy of the workers that created difficulties for the opposition. It was also its own recognition of economic realities. Its argument emphasised that the objective lack of resources would make life hard whatever policies were followed. It stressed both the need to develop industry internally and the necessity for the revolution to spread internationally as a means to doing this. But in the short term, it could offer little to the workers, even if a correct socialist policy was followed. When Trotsky and Preobrazhensky began to demand increased planning, they emphasised that this could not be done without squeezing the peasants and without the workers making sacrifices. The unified opposition of 'Trotskyists' and 'Zinovievists' in 1926 demanded as first priority certain improvements for the workers. But it was also realistic enough to denounce as utopian promises made to the workers by Stalin that far exceeded its own demands.

There is no space here to discuss the various platforms produced by the Left Opposition. But in outline they had three interlinked central planks.

1. The revolution could only make progress in a socialist direction if the economic weight of the towns as against the country, of industry as against agriculture, was increased. This demanded planning of industry and a policy of deliberately discriminating against the wealthy peasant in taxation policy. If this did not happen the latter would accumulate sufficient economic power to subordinate the state to his interests, thus producing a 'Thermidor', an internal counter-revolution.

2. This industrial development had to be accompanied by increased workers' democracy, so as to end bureaucratic tendencies in the party and state.

3. These first two policies could maintain Russia as a citadel of the revolution, but they could not produce that material and cultural level that is the prerequisite of socialism. This demanded the extension of the revolution abroad.

In purely economic terms, there was nothing impossible in this programme. Indeed its demand for planning of industrialisation and a squeezing of the peasants was eventually carried out—although in a manner which contradicted the intentions of the Opposition. But those who controlled the party from 1923 onwards did not see the wisdom of it. Only a severe economic crisis in 1928 forced them to plan and industrialise. For five years before this they persecuted the Left and expelled its leaders. The second plank in the programme they never implemented. As for the third plank, this had been Bolshevik orthodoxy in 1923,[13] only to be rejected by the party leaders for good in 1925.

It was not economics that prevented the party accepting this programme. It was rather the balance of social forces developing within the party itself. The programme demanded a break away from a tempo of production determined by the economic pressure of the peasantry. Two sorts of social forces had developed within the party that opposed this.

The 'Right' and the 'Centre'

The first was the simplest. This was made up of those elements who did not see concessions to the peasant as being detrimental to socialist construction. They consciously wanted the party to adjust its programme to the needs of the peasant. But this was not just a theoretical platform. It expressed the interest of all those in the party and state institutions who found co-operation with the peasants, including the *kulaks* and capitalist farmers, and the parasitic private traders who developed under NEP, the Nepmen, congenial. They found their theoretical expression in Bukharin, with his injunction to the peasants to 'enrich themselves'.

The second drew its strength as much from social forces within the party as outside. Its ostensible concern was to maintain social cohesion. As such it resisted the social tensions likely to be engendered if there was to be conscious effort to subordinate the country to the town, but did not go as far in its pro-peasant pronouncements as the right. In the main, it was constituted by elements within the party apparatus itself, whose whole orientation was to maintain party cohesion through bureaucratic means. Its leader was the chief of the party apparatus, Stalin.

To the Left Opposition at the time, the faction of Stalin seemed like a centrist group that oscillated between the traditions of the party (embodied in the Left programme) and the Right. In 1928 when Stalin suddenly adopted the first plank of the opposition's own programme, turning on the Right as viciously as he had only months before attacked the Left, and beginning industrialisation and the complete expropriation of the peasantry (so-called 'collectivisation'), this interpretation received a rude shock. Stalin clearly had a social base of his own. He could survive when neither the proletariat nor the peasantry exercised power.

If the Left Opposition was the result of groups motivated by the socialist and working-class traditions of the party attempting to embody these in realistic policies, and the Right opposition a result of accommodation to peasant pressures on the party, the successful Stalinist faction was based upon the party bureaucracy itself. This had begun life as a subordinate element within the social structure created by the revolution. It merely fulfilled certain elementary functions for the workers' party.

With the decimation of the working class in the civil war, the party was left standing above the class. In this situation the role of maintaining the cohesion of the party and state became central. Increasingly in the state and then in the party, this was provided by bureaucratic methods of control—often exercised by ex-Tsarist officials. The party apparatus increasingly exercised real power within the party—appointing functionaries at all levels, choosing delegates to conferences. But if it was the party and not the class that controlled the state and industry, then it was the party apparatus that increasingly inherited the gains the workers had made in the revolution.

The first result of this in terms of policies was a bureaucratic inertness. The bureaucrats of the apparatus offered a negative resistance to policies which might disturb their position. They began to act as a repressive force against any group that might challenge their position. Hence their opposition to the programmes of the Left and their refusal to permit any real discussion of them.

While the bureaucracy reacted in this negative way to threats of social disturbance, it quite naturally allied itself with the Right and Bukharin. This concealed its increasing existence as a social entity in its own right, with its own relationship to the means of production. Its repression of opposition in the party seemed to be an attempt to impose a pro-peasant policy on the party from above, not to be a part of its own struggle to remove any opposition to its own power in state and industry. Even after its proclamation of socialism in one country, its failures abroad seemed to flow more from bureaucratic inertia and the pro-peasant policies at home than from a conscious counter-revolutionary role.

Yet throughout this period the bureaucracy was developing from being a class in itself to being a class for itself. At the time of the inauguration of the NEP, it was objectively the case that power in the party and state lay in the hands of a small group of functionaries. But these were by no means a cohesive ruling class. They were far from being aware of sharing a common intent. The policies they implemented were shaped by elements in the party still strongly influenced by the traditions of revolutionary socialism. If at home objective conditions made workers' democracy nonexistent, at least there was the possibility of those motivated by the party's traditions bringing about its restoration given industrial recovery at home and revolution abroad.

Certainly on a world scale the party continued to play its revolutionary role. In its advice to foreign parties it made mistakes—and no doubt some of these flowed from its own bureaucratisation—but it did not commit crimes by subordinating them to its own national interests. Underlying the factional struggles of the 1920s is the process by which this social grouping shook off the heritage of the revolution to become a self-conscious class in its own right.

Counter-revolution

It is often said that the rise of Stalinism in Russia cannot be called 'counter-revolution' because it was a gradual process (for example Trotsky said that such a view involved 'winding back the film of reformism'). But this is to misconstrue the Marxist method. It is not the case that the transition from one sort of society to another always involves a single sudden change. This is the case for the transition from a capitalist state to a workers' state, because the working class cannot exercise its power except all at once, collectively, by a clash with the ruling class in which, as a culmination of long years of struggle, the latter's forces are defeated. But in the transition from feudalism to capitalism there are many cases in which there is not one sudden clash, but a whole series of different intensities and at different levels, as the decisive economic class (the bourgeoisie) forces political concessions in its favour.

The counter-revolution in Russia proceeded along the second path rather than the first. The bureaucracy did not have to seize power from the workers all at once. The decimation of the working class left power in its hands at all levels of Russian society. Its members controlled industry and the police and the army. It did not even have to wrest control of the state apparatus to bring it into line with its economic power, as the bourgeoisie did quite successfully in several countries without a sudden confrontation. It merely had to bring a political and industrial structure that it already controlled into line with its own interests.

This happened not 'gradually', but by a succession of qualitative changes by which the mode of operation of the party was brought into line with the demands of the central bureaucracy. Each of these qualitative changes could only be brought about by a direct confrontation with those elements in the party which, for whatever reason, still adhered to the revolutionary socialist tradition.

The first (and most important) such confrontation was that with the Left Opposition in 1923. Although the Opposition was by no means decisively and unambiguously opposed to what was happening to the party (for example, its leader, Trotsky, had made some of the most outrageously substitutionist statements during the trade-union debate of 1920; its first public statement—the Platform of the 46—was accepted by its signatories only with numerous reservations and amendments), the bureaucracy reacted to it with unprecedented hostility.

In order to protect its power the ruling group in the party resorted to methods of argument unheard of before in the Bolshevik Party. Systematic denigration of opponents replaced rational argument. The control of the secretariat of the party over appointments began to be used for the first time openly to remove sympathisers of the opposition from their posts (for example, the majority of the Komsomol youth organisation central committee were dismissed and sent to the provinces after some of them had replied to attacks on Trotsky).

To justify such procedures the ruling faction invented two new ideological entities, which it counterposed to one another. On the one hand it inaugurated a cult of 'Leninism' (despite the protests of Lenin's widow). It attempted to elevate Lenin to a semi-divine status by mummifying his dead body in the manner of the Egyptian pharaohs. On the other, it invented 'Trotskyism' as a tendency opposed to Leninism, justifying this with odd quotations from Lenin of ten or even twenty years before, while ignoring Lenin's last statement (his 'Testament') that referred to Trotsky as 'the most able member of the central committee' and suggested the removal of Stalin.

The leaders of the party perpetrated these distortions and falsifications consciously in order to fight off any threat to their control of the party

(Zinoviev, at the time the leading member of the 'triumvirate', later admitted this). In doing so, one section of the party was showing that it had come to see its own power as more important than the socialist tradition of free inner-party discussion. By reducing theory to a mere adjunct of its own ambitions, the party bureaucracy was beginning to assert its identity as against other social groups.

The second major confrontation began in a different way. It was not at first a clash between members of the party with socialist aspirations and the increasingly powerful bureaucracy itself. It began as a clash between the ostensible leader of the party (at the time, Zinoviev) and the party apparatus that really controlled. In Leningrad Zinoviev controlled a section of the bureacracy to a considerable extent independently of the rest of the apparatus. Although its mode of operation was in no way different from that prevailing throughout the rest of the country, its very independence was an obstacle to the central bureaucracy. It represented a possible source of policies and activities that might disturb the overall rule of the bureaucracy. For this reason it had to be brought within the ambit of the central apparatus.

In the process Zinoviev was forced from his leading position in the party. Having lost this, he began to turn once more to the historical traditions of Bolshevism and to the policies of the Left (although he never lost fully his desire to be part of the ruling bloc, continually wavering for the next ten years between the Left and the apparatus).

With the fall of Zinoviev, power lay in the hands of Stalin, who with his unrestrained use of bureaucratic methods of control of the party, his disregard for theory, his hostility to the traditions of the revolution in which his own role had been a minor one, his willingness to resort to any means to dispose of those who had actually led the revolution, above all epitomised the growing self-consciousness of the apparatus.

All these qualities he exhibited to their full extent in the struggle against the new opposition. Meetings were 'packed', speakers shouted down, prominent oppositionists likely to find themselves assigned to minor positions in remote areas, former Tsarist officers utilised as *agents provocateurs* to discredit oppositional groups. Eventually, in 1928, Stalin began to imitate the Tsars directly and deport revolutionaries to Siberia. In the long run, even this was not to be enough. He was to do what even the Romanoffs had been unable to do: systematically murder those who had constituted the revolutionary party of 1917.

By 1928 the Stalinist faction had completely consolidated its control in the party and state. When Bukharin and the right wing split from it, horrified by what they had helped to create, they found themselves with even less strength than the Left Oppositions had.

But the party was not in control of the whole of Russian society. The towns, where real power lay, were still surrounded by the sea of peasant production. The bureaucracy had usurped the gains of the working class in the revolution, but so far the peasantry remained unaffected. A mass refusal of the peasants to sell their grain in 1928 brought this home sharply to the bureaucracy.

What followed was the assertion of the power of the towns over the countryside that the Left Opposition had been demanding for years. This led certain oppositionists (Preobrazhensky and Radek, for example) to make their peace with Stalin. Yet this policy was in its spirit the opposite of that of the Left. They had argued the need to subordinate peasant production to worker-owned industry in the towns. But industry in the towns was no longer worker-owned. It was under the control of the bureaucracy that held the state. Assertion of the domination of the town over the country was now the assertion not of the working class over the peasantry, but of the bureaucracy over the last part of society lying outside its control.

It imposed this dominance with all the ferocity ruling classes have always used. Not only *kulaks*, but all grades of peasants, whole villages of peasants, suffered. The 'Left' turn of 1928 finally liquidated the revolution of 1917 in town and country.

There can be no doubt that by 1928 a new class had taken power in Russia. It did not have to engage in direct military conflict with the workers to gain power, because direct workers' power had not existed since 1918. But it did have to purge the party, which had been left in power, of all those who retained links, however tenuous, with the socialist tradition. When a reinvigorated working class confronted it again, whether in Berlin or Budapest in the 1950s, or in Russia itself (for example at Novo-Cherkassk in 1962), it used the tanks it had not needed in 1928.

The Left Opposition was far from clear about what it was fighting. Trotsky, to his dying day, believed that the apparatus that was to hunt him down and murder him was a degenerated workers' state. Yet it was that Opposition alone which fought day by day against the destruction by the Stalinist apparatus of the revolution at home and prevention of revolution abroad.[14] For a whole historical period it alone resisted the distorting effects on the socialist movement of Stalinism and Social Democracy. Its own theories about Russia made this task more difficult, but it still carried it out. That is why today any genuinely revolutionary movement must place itself in that tradition.

THREE

THE NATURE
OF STALINIST RUSSIA
AND THE EASTERN BLOC

CHRIS HARMAN

IN 1917 for the first time in history a workers' government took control of a major country. To millions throughout a world locked in a savage and futile war it offered new hope. In the years afterwards people everywhere turned from the grim alternatives of a declining capitalism—unemployment, poverty, fascist barbarity, the threat of new wars—to place their hopes for the future in the new society born of the revolution.

Yet today the USSR inspires support from few on the left. From the Moscow trials and the Stalin-Hitler Pact in the 1930s to the brutal and bloody suppression of the Hungarian revolution in 1956 its actions turned thousands of militants against it. Even the official Communist Parties of the West protested, albeit in a half-hearted fashion, against the invasion and occupation of Czechoslovakia. Meanwhile the treatment of China—from withdrawing much-needed technical aid to threatening war over a few barren border areas—has disillusioned those who even today manage to praise Stalin.

For more than forty years attempts to come to terms with what has happened in Russia, to understand why the hopes of 1917 were not realised, and to explain the dynamics of the society that took its place, have occupied a central place in all socialist discussions.

First published as 'The Eastern Bloc' in N Harris and J Palmer (editors), *World Crisis* (London 1971).

These problems have if anything increased since the years of the Second World War as a dozen or more countries have witnessed the establishment of societies more or less similar to that of Russia.

October

The revolution of October 1917 was clearly and unequivocally made by the industrial working class. Although it has often been argued since by opponents of the Bolsheviks, whether from the anarchist left or from the social democrat or liberal right, that the working class played little or no role, and that Lenin seized power with an autocratically run party, without the workers or over their heads, facts just will not bear out such arguments. As one of the most prominent opponents of the Bolsheviks, Martov, wrote at the time:

> Understand, please, what we have before us after all is a victorious uprising of the proletariat—almost the entire proletariat supports Lenin and expects its social liberation from the uprising . . . [1]

In fact, far from being small and operating in detachment from the mass of workers, the Bolshevik Party was a mass organisation with 176,000 members in July 1917[2] and 260,000 members at the beginning of 1918.[3] Since there were a mere two million workers employed in factories undergoing inspection[4] something approaching 10 per cent of the working class must have been members of the Bolshevik Party immediately after the 'July days'—at a time when the party was virtually illegal and its leaders in hiding or in prison.

Nor is there any truth in the claim that the party was 'autocratically run' or even 'totalitarian'. Free debate, in which the whole party, and on occasion even workers outside the party, took part, was an integral feature both in 1917 and afterwards right up to the tenth party congress of 1921.[5]

Finally, the revolution itself was far from being a coup establishing a totalitarian or autocratic regime. Rather it replaced a provisional government, that was responsible to no one, by one freely chosen by the workers' and soldiers' delegates assembled at the Second Congress of the Soviets—summoned there by an anti-Bolshevik executive.[6] In the months after October, different parties continued to debate freely in the soviets. Even at the height of civil war in 1919 the Mensheviks, for instance, were still allowed to publish propaganda.

Ten years after

By 1927 little remained of the proletarian democracy of 1917. But this could hardly be blamed on those who took power in October. For during a long and bitter struggle against counter-revolution and foreign invasion the working class that had made the revolution was itself decimated. Cut off from its sources of raw materials, industry ground to a prolonged halt. By 1920 industrial production had fallen to about 18 per cent of what it had been in 1916. The number of workers employed was about half of the 1916 figure. These workers could not keep alive on what their collective product would buy. Many had to resort to direct barter with peasants—exchanging their products, or even parts of their machines, for food.

Large numbers of workers were at the front. Here, dispersed among a peasant army over a vast area, they could hardly exercise immediate and direct control over the soviet apparatus in the cities. The best and most militant of them were those likely to bear the burden of the fighting and to suffer the greatest casualties. Those who survived would return from the army not as workers but as commissars and administrators in the army and in the state machine. Their place in the factories would be taken by raw peasants from the countryside without socialist traditions or aspirations.

The Bolshevik Party had come to power as the most conscious section of a mass working-class uprising; it was left holding power, although the working class itself hardly existed by 1920. If the regime was still in some ways socialist, it was not because of its social base but because those who made decisions at the top still had socialist aspirations.

As Lenin wrote: 'It must be recognised that the party's proletarian policy is determined at present not by its rank and file, but by the immense and undivided authority of the tiny sections that might be called the party's "old guard".'[7]

In order to hold together the country after the decimation of the class that had made the revolution, the Bolshevik old guard were forced to employ various bureaucratic methods. They had no choice but to try to build a reliable state apparatus. To man this they were forced to utilise what in many cases were the only personnel at hand with the required skills, members of the old Tsarist bureaucracy. But they shared none of the aspirations of 1917 and were accustomed to diametrically opposed methods in dealing with the mass of the people. Such methods and attitudes were bound to influence Bolshevik Party members working alongside them. Lenin was acutely aware of this:

> Let us look at Moscow. Who is leading whom? The 4,700 responsible communists, the mass of bureacrats, or the other way round? I do not seriously think you can say the communists are leading this mass. To be honest they are not the leaders but the led.[8]

As Lenin was dying it became clear that even the top leadership of the party was not immune to the influences that were eating away at the rest of the party. Lenin's last political act was to argue for the removal of Stalin as party secretary because of crudely bureaucratic behaviour in relation to other party members. In the years that followed, the authoritarian methods that had entered the lower ranks of the party from its environment were used to eliminate from the leadership those who challenged the prevailing bureaucratic approach. First, Trotsky and the Left Opposition were subject to a torrent of systematic abuse of a kind that had never previously characterised discussion inside the Bolshevik Party. A year later the followers of Zinoviev and Kamenev were to receive the same treatment. Expulsion from the party and a police-enforced deportation to remote areas was to follow, and finally imprisonment for those who did not recant. The same fate was to await the last source of disagreement—the 'Right Opposition' of Bukharin and Tomsky.

The decimation of the working class in the civil war had left power with the Bolshevik Party in the absence of the class that party represented. In order to rule in such a situation, the party had no choice but to call into being a massive bureaucracy. It was the members of this that objectively controlled the state and the means of industrial production.

But the decisions taken and the policies implemented still flowed in part from the subjective intentions of those at the top of the party, who had spent their whole lives fighting for the working class. The factional struggles in the party in the 1920s were not so much struggles for different policies as a struggle between those who ran the central bureaucratic apparatus and those who had led the party through the revolution. In this struggle those who ran the apparatus began to define their own interests in opposition to the revolutionary socialist tradition of October. In a series of key confrontations they broke decisively with that tradition, qualitatively changing the functioning of the party and state, physically forcing out of its ranks those who adhered, however inconsistently, to those traditions.

Firstly there was the elimination of the elementary preconditions of scientific debate in the struggle against the Left Opposition, then the removal of any alternative sources of policy-making or propaganda in the struggle against the 'Leningrad Opposition' of Zinoviev and the abandonment of all the traditions of socialist internationalism with the slogan of 'socialism in one country', finally, with the use of force against dissidents, the end of any pretence of free discussion.

By 1929 those who had been part of the party that made the revolution had, with only one or two exceptions, been removed from effective influence over events. They were replaced by men whose role in the revolution had been insignificant—the second-order functionaries that had manned the apparatus of the Bolshevik Party, those who had passed over to Bolshevism from Menshevism after the revolution, the new breed of bureaucrats that had multiplied in the 1920s. These new rulers finally celebrated their victory in the Moscow trials, when they physically liquidated the party of 1917—not just the followers of Trotsky, Zinoviev and Bukharin, but also those who had collaborated with Stalin and the apparatus on their road to power.*

Since it was the old guard, not a confident, self-active working class that safeguarded the traditions of the revolution and ensured their transformation into socialist policies, the defeat of the old guard was a defeat of the revolution itself.

The controllers of the apparatus already controlled industry and the forces of the state by 1923. Certainly there was not a working class controlling these in the ways Lenin had outlined in writing *State and Revolution*. But the bureaucrats did not yet rule in a conscious manner, aware of interests of their own. In Marx's terms they were a 'class in themselves', a collection of individuals occupying a similar relationship to the means of production, not yet a 'class for itself', a group aware of

---

* At the seventeenth party congress in 1934 40 per cent of the delegates had been in the party since before the revolution and 80 per cent from 1919 or earlier; by the eighteenth congress of 1939 only 5 per cent had been members since before the revolution and only 14 per cent since before 1919. Again, in 1939, although it has been estimated that something approaching 200,000 members of the Bolshevik Party of 1918 must have been alive, there were only 20,000 or 10 per cent of them left in the party.[9]

its common interests and acting together as an independent historical force to achieve these.

Between 1923 and 1929 this ruling group became aware of their separate interests, opposed to those of the working class embodied in the traditions of 1917 and personified by the old guard, in the main in a negative sense. They feared and fought against any perspective that might disturb their positions of bureaucratic privilege and make life harder for themselves. Their chief characteristic was inertia and complacency. At home it meant acquiescing to pressures from the peasantry; abroad subordinating foreign Communist parties to the need to ensure international security for the Soviet Union. Both policies were justified by the slogan of 'Socialism in One Country', with its quietist implication that there would be 'growing into' socialism without convulsion or much conscious effort by the apparatus.

In this period, although the Russian state was no longer anything like 'the state which is not a state', the 'commune state', the 'workers' state' of Lenin's *State and Revolution*, neither did it aim at goals diametrically opposed to those of the mass of workers. Policy was directed less and less by the revolutionary programme of Bolshevism, but not yet by some clearly articulated alternative. The men of the apparatus were extending their control over all potential sources of power and were more and more becoming aware of their own distinct interests, but they had not yet fully defined these. As a result policies seemed to drift in this direction or that, depending upon various pressures exerted: the acquiescence to the peasants in the countryside, the pressures from the trade union apparatus, the need to outflank a particular demand of the opposition, the need to prove the opposition wrong, the interests of this or that particular section of the apparatus.

There was still a sense in which the state could be called a 'workers' state', although a 'degenerate' one, as Trotsky called it. For the interests of the workers still influenced the formation of policy.[10] In the factories the *troika* of manager, trade union and workers still functioned to some extent, with managerial directives being influenced by the trade union committees and the Communist workers.

Workers still had the right to strike and exercised this (although to a diminishing extent). A third of strikes were settled in their interests. Trade union functionaries showed some concern for the needs of their members and engaged in collective bargaining with the employers.[11] Real wages showed a long-term tendency to rise in this period to at least pre-war levels.[12] Although the bureaucrats were tightening their grip on the last sources of power and eliminating any opposition, their policies still reflected some of the interests of the workers (just as the most bureaucratic independent trade union in the capitalist countries does). One index of this was that until 1929 the wage of a party member, whatever his employment, was restricted to the same level as that of the skilled worker.

1929

At the end of 1928 the policies of the Russian leadership suddenly underwent a dramatic reversal. For five years Stalin, with Bukharin and Tomsky, had been arguing against the criticisms of the Left Opposition, who held that the rate of industrial growth was too slow and that the policy towards the countryside was strengthening the *kulaks*, who would eventually use their strength to attack the regime.[13] In 1928 these predictions were validated when there was a massive spontaneous refusal of the peasants to sell their grain to the state. Stalin and his supporters then turned on Bukharin and Tomsky and began to implement policies apparently similar to ones previously opposed.

In fact Stalin began 'attacking the *kulaks*' and carrying through industrialisation on a scale never dreamt of by the Left Opposition. Armed detachments were sent into the countryside to procure quantities of grain needed to feed the growing population of the towns. The same forces 'encouraged' the peasants to pool their land in 'collectives'. This occurred at a speed that Stalin could not have predicted. The First Five Year Plan of the end of 1928 only estimated 20 per cent collectivisation in five years—the actual rate was to be at least 60 per cent. In order to achieve this, a veritable civil war had to be fought in the countryside, in which millions of peasants—and not all of them *kulaks*—died.

The purpose of the collectivisation was both to destroy the economic power of the peasantry and to pump foodstuffs and raw materials from the countryside to the towns where they could feed a growing industrial workforce, without having to give the peasants manufactured goods in return. Even though collectivisation did not lead to an increase in total agricultural production (in the early 1950s this was hardly higher than before the First World War) and led to a catastrophic decline in the production of many foodstuffs, it enabled the bureaucracy to get more grain off the peasants by reducing the level of consumption.

The industrialisation plans of the Left Opposition which had been severely criticised by Stalin had called for a rate of industrial growth of less than 20 per cent per year. By 1930 Stalin was talking about a rate of growth of 40 per cent.

In this reversal of party policy, not only did the peasants lose what they had gained from the revolution—ownership of the land—but the conditions of the workers rapidly deteriorated. In September 1929 regulations were introduced radically reducing the powers of the *troika* in the factories. '. . . The adoption of the plan ended the period during which the trade unions had, with increasing difficulty, enjoyed a certain independence within the Soviet economy.'[14] In accordance with the new policy, strikes were no longer permitted or even reported in the press. Nor, from the end of 1930 on, were workers allowed to change jobs without permission.[15]

The average wages of workers and employees were cut over the seven-year period from 1929 on by anything up to 50 per cent.[16] At the same time wage differentials were sharply increased, and the rule restricting the earnings of party members to that of skilled workers was modified. Meanwhile the system of forced labour was introduced for the first time. The number of those in penal camps jumped from thirty thousand in 1928 to 662,257 in 1930. In the next few years this figure was to rise to somewhere in the region of five million or more.[17]

Until 1928 the state and industrial apparatus pursued policies that expressed a combination of the interests of its bureaucratic controllers, and the pressures of workers and peasants on it. From 1929 it began to act in a clear and determined manner to pursue policies that undermined the conditions of life of both workers and peasants. Economic policy no longer drifted this way and that because of various forces at work which articulated arguments for their point of view. It moved decisively in one direction, with a seeming dynamic of its own. Yet this hardly seems to have been one consciously arrived at. 'Down to that time [the spring of 1929], debates were conducted in the leading party organs on major issues of policy . . . though the free expression of opinions hostile to the party was increasingly restricted. This—almost suddenly—ceases to be true after the spring of 1929.'[18] That is to say, the goals of policy were no longer a matter for conscious debate and choice. They were now taken for granted without argument, as if they were imposed from outside by some unchangeable alien force. This continues to be the case today—and not just for Russia, but also for the other Communist states.

The task that any theory that attempts to interpret Stalinism must set itself to locate this dynamic.

The Soviet Union and the world economy

In the early years of the revolution it had been an almost self-evident truth to all the Bolshevik leaders that the relatively small working class in Russia would not be able to hold power for long, let alone develop the advanced forces of production needed to overcome scarcity and build socialism, without assistance from successful revolutions in the advanced capitalist countries. In 1924 Stalin and Bukharin revised this doctrine to suit the new mood of the apparatus. They argued that socialism could be built in backward Russia at 'snail's pace' through a policy of making concessions to the peasantry. To this end there should be a slow but steady increase in production of consumer goods from light industry, which would then encourage the peasant to produce more grain and send it to the town.

This policy of 'socialism in one country' corresponded to the interests of a whole stratum of bureaucrats who feared the risks to their own position that any struggle against the peasants at home or any international revolutionary events abroad might entail. It meant subordinating everything to their personal inertia.

The Left Opposition argued that such a policy could only lead to the defeat of the revolution in the long term, for in reality there were superior productive forces at the disposal of the capitalist powers that could lead to the downfall of the revolution, through either direct military action, or through subversion of the revolution as the prospect of cheap foreign goods appealed to bourgeois elements, peasants, and sections of the party. As one of the leaders of the Opposition, Smilga, put it in 1926: 'We must orient ourselves on our own resources; we must act like a country that does not wish to turn into a colony, we must force the industrialisation of the economy.'[19] The conclusion, the need for industrialisation, however, was not regarded as making possible the building of socialism but merely the defence of the revolution until it should spread abroad.

The Opposition was concerned that industrialisation should proceed so as to safeguard and extend the gains of the revolution. That is why they linked it to the demands for improved conditions for the workers, an extension of workers' democracy and a struggle against bureaucracy, and to a consistent revolutionary international orientation. Until 1928 the major task for the bureaucracy was to combat such dangerous challenges to its own position. But once its own control over the state and industry was assured against any disturbance from the Left, the arguments for industrialisation began to appeal to at least a section of the apparatus.

Industrialisation would mean both increasing its power vis-à-vis other classes in Russian society—particularly the peasants—and protecting its control over Russian industry from foreign threats.

The defence of Russia, however, particularly if there was no belief in the possibility or necessity of revolution abroad, meant shifting the emphasis in industrial development from light industry, that could produce goods for which peasants would voluntarily exchange their food products, to heavy industry. A shift in this direction began to take place from the middle of 1927. Following a heightening of international tension those sections of the party around Stalin began to declare that 'we must tie in plans for industrial development more closely with the defence capacity of our country.'[20] In the months that followed there was an increased emphasis on the development of industry. This shift began to create further interests in the apparatus concerned with industrialisation. 'The drive for further expansion came as much from officials and managers—many of them now party members—as from party leaders.'[21]

This development of heavy industry was not yet at anything like the rate it was to reach from 1929 on. But it did signify the opening up of divisions within the bureaucracy, between those for whom what mattered was an easy life through acquiescence to peasant and worker pressures and those who saw their own long-term interests as being more important, identifying these with the development of heavy industry, regardless of the consequences. The refusal of the peasants to supply grain to the towns in 1928–29 put the whole plan for industrialisation in danger. The only way of placating them would have been to accept the arguments of Bukharin and Tomsky and subordinate the development of heavy industry, and therefore of modern weaponry, to the demand of the peasants for consumer goods. This difference of interests within the bureaucracy became a complete split, with the majority then turning on both the peasants and workers and developing heavy industry at their expense.

In order to achieve this development, the consumer goods industries were hardly developed at all. While in 1927–28 only 32.8 per cent of industrial investment took the form of means of production (as against

55.7 per cent means of consumption), by 1932 this had grown to 53.3 per cent, from which level it was to rise continuously until it reached 68.8 per cent in 1950. In other words, everything—above all, the living standards of workers and collective farmers—was subordinated to the production of means of production used to produce other means of production. Industry grew, but living standards deteriorated.[22] Stalin himself made clear the motive behind these policies:

> To slacken the pace [of industrialisation] would mean to lag behind; and those who lag behind are beaten. We do not want to be beaten. No we don't want to. The history of old Russia . . . she was ceaselessly beaten for her backwardness . . . by the Monghol Khans, . . . by Turkish Beys, . . . by Polish-Lithuanian Panz, . . . by Anglo-French capitalists, . . . by Japanese barons, she was beaten by all—for her backwardness, for military backwardness, for cultural backwardness, for political backwardness, for industrial backwardness, for agricultural backwardness . . . We are fifty or a hundred years behind the advanced countries. We must make good this lag in ten years. Either we do it or they crush us.[23]

Or again:

> The environment in which we are placed . . . at home and abroad . . . compels us to adopt a rapid rate of growth of our industry.[24]

For the section of the bureaucracy around Stalin the collectivisation and industrialisation, the subordination of consumption to an accumulation of means of production, no longer seemed like a question upon which an arbitrary choice could be made. It had become a question of life or death to them. Either there was accumulation or the 'environment' abroad would crush them. Accumulation had to take place so that Russia, their Russia, the Russia that they owned through their control over the state and industrial apparatus, a Russia readily identifiable with the Russia of the tsars in speeches such as Stalin's quoted above, could be defended against attack. If accumulation did not produce consumer goods for the working population of Russia, it did produce the weapons to ensure that the bureaucracy would not lose the means of production it controlled to international imperialism.

In fact, the Stalinist bureaucracy was responding to the same choice that every non-capitalist ruling class throughout the world faced from the second quarter of the nineteenth century onwards. As industrial capitalism developed in Western Europe and North America, extending its tentacles so as to drain resources from the remotest areas of the globe, it threatened the position of all existing ruling classes. Everywhere it tried to replace their rule by its rule, or at least to reduce them to the level of being its continually humiliated agents. And given the unprecedented growth of the means of production under capitalism, together with the concentration of the major part of the earth's resources in the hands of the rulers of metropolitan capitalism, the means—military and economic—were available to bring this about.

The only way that existing ruling classes could resist this subjection was to change radically their own mode of exploitation of the local population. All pre-capitalist societies are characterised by one feature: however great the extent of exploitation of the mass of the population, it is determined by the consumption needs of the ruling class. The main function of exploitation is to allow the ruling class and its hangers-on to live in luxury. The actual extent and efficiency of exploitation is therefore to a certain extent accidental, depending upon the desires of the ruler, as well as the extent of the resistance of the oppressed. As Marx put it, 'the walls of the lord's stomach determine the limits of the exploitation of the serf'. Any improvement in the general level of culture or any advance in the forces of production is an accidental by-product of the consumption of the ruling class. Thus, for instance, in imperial China, the peasants were as exploited as much as possible, but the result was merely to enable a massive bureaucracy to live in luxury, not to develop the means of production, except intermittently and accidentally.

Under capitalism, on the other hand, however high the luxury consumption of the ruling class, this is not the motive force of the system. In order to safeguard his own position, each entrepreneur has continually to invest a large amount of his profits in new means of production. Only in this way can he reduce his costs of production and prevent any rival from undercutting him on the market. At the same time and for the same reason, he has continually to keep close watch on the actual process of exploitation so as to ensure that his wage costs are at a minimum. In order to survive, the capitalist has continually to expand production at the expense of consumption. Production in the interests of further production, accumulation in the interests of further accumulation, are the motive forces of capitalism, not as with pre-capitalist societies (and also, incidentally, socialist society) production and accumulation in the interests of consumption. As Marx wrote:

> Except as personified capital, the capitalist has no historical value, and no right to that historical existence . . . But so far as he is personified in capital, it is not values in use and the enjoyment of them that spurs him to action, but exchange value and its augmentation that spur him into action. Fanatically bent on making value expand itself, he ruthlessly forces the human race to produce for production's sake; . . . so far, therefore, as his actions are a mere function of capital his own private consumption is a robbery perpetrated on accumulation . . . Therefore, save, save, i.e. reconvert the greatest possible portion of surplus value or surplus product into capital! Accumulation for accumulation's sake, production for production's sake.[25]

This continual accumulation provides capitalism with the means to guarantee success in its attempt to subdue other societies. Unless, that is, the ruling classes of these societies can change the basis on which they themselves rule. They can only protect themselves if they can develop the forces of production at a comparable rate to that of the established capitalisms (or, actually, since they start in the race later, at a faster rate). In other words, if they too can change their mode of exploitation so as to subordinate everything else to the accumulation of means of production in order to accumulate other means of production, they can protect themselves from an expanding capitalism—if they can transform themselves so as successfully to imitate the absurd rationality of that capitalism.

In the nineteenth century various ruling classes attempted to protect themselves in this way. Thus there was an early but unsuccessful attempt to transform an oriental despotic Egypt in this manner. In tsarist Russia the regime encouraged the development of industry. In Japan alone, however, was the attempt fully successful. For hundreds of years the Japanese ruling class had tried artificially to cut the country off from foreign penetration (a policy of 'feudalism in one country'). In the 1860s the arrival of an American gunboat proved the futility of such a policy unless there were the productive forces to manufacture armaments to back it up. At this point a section of that ruling class carried through the Meiji Restoration, by which it took control of the state and used this control to subordinate the whole of Japanese society to the development of industry on a capitalist basis.

In 1929 the Stalinist ruling stratum in Russia faced exactly the same dilemma: follow the logic of capitalism and accumulate in order to further accumulate or face subjection to international capitalism. The only other alternative was that of the Left Opposition, of undermining the basis of this dilemma by subordinating internal developments in Russia to the needs of spreading the revolution abroad (and given the social convulsions that did take place in the 1930s—in Germany, in France, in Spain, this was not an absurd perspective. Certainly if the policies of the International Left Opposition had been followed by the Communist Parties of these countries, there would have been a strong possibility of success). But this alternative was one which the bureaucratic stratum ruling Russia could not accept because it would have undermined its own privileged position.

Forced industrialisation and the collectivisation of the peasantry were the only ways the bureaucratic ruling stratum knew of defending itself. But in order to carry these through, it had to turn upon every other class in Russian society, to subordinate them to its needs of accumulation. That is why the year of inauguration of the five-year 'plans' was the year of the abolition of independent trade unions, of the abolition of the right to strike, the year when for the first time wages were forced downwards by the bureaucracy. It also meant that the bureaucracy itself had to be transformed from a coalition of different privileged interests into a homogeneous class, dedicated to the single goal of accumulation, in which no degree of free discussion over objectives remained.

Russia—state capitalist

There is a tendency for people to identify capitalism with one or other of its superficial characteristics—the stock exchange,[26] periodic economic crises, unemployment, 'thirst for profits',[27] or the 'final money form of capital'.[28] They quite naturally conclude that because such characteristics do not exist in Russia then that country cannot be a variant of capitalism. Marx, on the other hand, was concerned not with these external aspects, but with the underlying dynamic of capitalism that produced these. This he located in two basic features.

1. That each individual act of labour is related to each other, not by conscious planning, but by an unplanned and anarchic comparison of the products of that labour. In this way each commodity has its price determined by the proportion of the total labour of society needed to produce

it. '. . . The different kinds of private labour, which are being carried on independently of each other . . . are continually being reduced to the quantitative proportions in which society requires them . . .'[29] The 'relation of producers to the sum total of their labour is presented to them as a social relation, existing not between themselves, but between the products of their labour.'[30] Thus, the labour of individuals is related in a quantitative fashion to the labour of all other individuals in society by the relations that come to exist between the products of their labour. This in turn means that each production process is determined by factors outside itself, that is by the relation of its costs to those of production taking place elsewhere. There is 'regulation of mutual production by the costs of production . . . the product is related to itself as a realisation of determined quantity of general labour, of social labour time.'[31] The methods of production of each producer have continually to be changed as there are unplanned and anarchic changes in the methods of all other producers.

2. There is a separation of producers from the means of production. Workers can then only survive by selling their own ability to work (their 'labour power') to those who own the means of production. The price they receive (in other words their wages) will be continually reduced by their mutual interaction to the cost of production of this labour power, that is to the historically and culturally determined level of subsistence for themselves and their families.

These two factors together produce a situation in which rival owners of means of production are producing goods in competition with one another. Each can use the surplus obtained through exploitation to develop the means of production, so increasing production and lowering costs, thereby forcing out of business rivals unless they do likewise. Each, therefore, has to try to resist the inroads of the other by expanding the means of production controlled.

> That which in the miser is a mere idiosyncrasy, is in the capitalist the effect of the social mechanism of which he is but one of the cogs. Moreover, the development of capitalist production makes it constantly necessary to keep increasing the amount of capital laid out in a given industrial undertaking, and competition makes the immanent laws of capitalist production to be felt by each individual capitalist as external coercive laws. It compels him to keep constantly expanding his capital in order to preserve it, but extend it he cannot except by means of accumulation.[32]

This relationship between different accumulations of alienated labour (the means of production) defines each as *capital* for Marx and their owners as *capitalists*. It also determines the interactions of capitalists with one another and with their workers, so as continually to reproduce the competition.

Now when Marx describes the mechanisms whereby different accumulations of alienated labour are compared with each other, he talks in terms of the mechanisms of the market. But in principle there is no reason why other mechanisms which relate independent acts of production to one another in an unplanned manner should not play the same role. Any process by which the organisation of production is continually being transformed through comparison with production taking place elsewhere in an unplanned fashion will have the same results.

In fact, as capitalism develops, the direct role of the market in relating different processes of production tends to diminish. As Hilferding wrote sixty years ago: 'The realisation of the Marxian theory of concentration—the monopoly merger—seems to lead to the invalidation of the Marxian law of value.'[33]

Within the giant firm deliberate, planned decisions of the management, not the direct impact of the market, seem to determine the allocation of resources, the wages of workers, the speed of the production process at each individual point. These decisions are not taken in a vacuum, however. Even the largest of the giant firms has to worry about competition on an *international* scale. It can survive only so long as it can expand at the expense of its rivals. Although the conditions under which each separate item is produced need not necessarily be competitive, overall production has to be. The anarchy of the international market still determines the tyranny of the firm.

With the development of a war economy or a permanent arms economy, the direct role of the market diminishes still more. The typical situation for a large proportion of the economy is of the monopoly firm producing for a single buyer—the government—at a price determined by the decisions of the latter.

> When capitalists work for defence, i.e. for the government treasury, it is obviously no more 'pure' capitalism, but a special form of national economy. Pure capitalism means commodity production. Commodity production means working for an unknown and free market. But the capitalist 'working' for defence does not 'work' for the market at all.[34]

But the Marxian law of value does still operate—insofar as the government, responding to various pressures upon itself, consciously attempts to relate the price it pays for arms to the costs of producing goods elsewhere. The government consciously decides on prices; to this extent the market plays no role. But the government makes its decisions in accordance with the level of costs of production in society as a whole so that every change in costs elsewhere in the economy will eventually have its effect on the process of arms production. In other words the government forces the arms-producing firm to behave as if it did confront the market. The government imposes the law of value on the firm.

Should it fail to do so the consequences are clear. Either a greater proportion of national resources are devoted to arms production than is the case with foreign rivals, therefore (through taxes, inflation of raw material costs, and so on) making non-arms-producing firms uncompetitive in international markets; or there is insufficient development of military potential, so that the national ruling class loses out in physical confrontations with its competitors. Again the international market imposes discipline in the long run.

Since 1929 the Russian economy has been subordinated to needs arising out of its interaction with the capitalist West. This has not in the main taken the form of direct market competition.[35] But there has been a mediating mechanism between the Russian economy and the economies of the capitalist West that has played a similar role to that of direct market competition: competition through arms production. As we have shown above, what motivated the Stalinist bureaucracy when it first began systematically to build up heavy industry at the expense of light industry and the living standards of workers and peasants was its fear of losing out in military competition with Western rulers. The ability of the Western rulers to threaten Russia was based on a development of industry through the continued extraction of surplus value. Stalin, in order to be able to produce armaments of similar level, was forced to try to develop a similar level of heavy industry. This he could only do, given the low level of industrialisation of Russia, by actually pumping a surplus out of the Russian population at a greater rate than that extracted in the West.

Competition between capitalists in the West forces each to reduce the level of consumption of their workers to a historically and culturally determined minimum and to accumulate capital. Competition with the

West forces the Russian bureaucracy to reduce wage levels inside Russia to a historically and culturally determined minimum in a similar way.

Many Western socialists have tried to ignore such realities. The bureaucratic rulers of Russia, however, do have some idea of the forces impelling them to act in a certain way; for instance, *Pravda* (24 April 1970) reported a speech in which

> Comrade Brezhnev dwelt on the question of the economic competition between the two world systems. 'This competition takes different forms,' he said. 'In many cases we are coping successfully with the task of overtaking and outdistancing the capitalist countries in the production of certain types of output . . . but the fundamental question is not only how much you produce but also at what cost, with what outlays of labour . . . It is in this field that the centre of gravity between the two systems lies in our time.'

This is not a once and for all process. The very success of the Russian bureaucracy in developing heavy industry and arms production becomes a force compelling accumulation in the West, which in turn compels further accumulation inside Russia. In other words, a total system of 'reified' relations is set up in which the anarchic and unplanned interaction of the products of labour determines the labour process.

> The object which labour produces confronts it as something alien, as a power independent of the producer . . . The worker is related to the product of his labour as to an alien object . . . The more the worker spends himself, the more powerful the alien world becomes which he creates over against himself . . . The worker puts his life into the object; but now his life no longer belongs to himself but to his object.[36]

Marx's classic description of alienation applies as much to Russia as to the capitalist West.

And so does the feature which above all makes capitalism a distinct mode of production for the mature Marx: that whereas under pre-capitalist societies production is determined by the desires of the ruling class and under socialism by the desires of the mass of the population, under capitalism the nature and dynamic of production results from the compulsion on those who control production to extract a surplus in order to accumulate means of production in competition with one another. The particular way in which the ruling class owns industry in Russia, through its control of the state, does not affect this essential point. That is why the only meaningful designation in Marxist terms for the society that has existed in Russia for the last forty years* is 'state capitalism.'

The Stalin period

Not only the mass of workers, peasants and slave labourers suffered as everything inside Russia was subordinated to the building up of heavy industry. Within the bureaucracy itself a reign of terror operated. Those who had any scruples about the exploitation of the rest of the population were imprisoned, exiled, tortured and finally executed during the great purges. The last furtive remnants of Bolshevism in the state and party apparatus were eradicated.[37] Anyone who might conceivably act to impede the extraction of a surplus and its transformation into means of production was eliminated. Fear of what would happen should there be a failure to meet demands from above had to be great enough to counteract pressures from workers and peasants below. This had its corollary in the enforcement of a monolithic political line: any discussion within the bureaucracy might easily come to reflect the repressed aspirations of the exploited masses outside. Hence the continual and seemingly absurd exactions of the police apparatus.

Yet it was not just fear that made for stability during the Stalin period. For however much the individual suffered from the terror, however great the continual paranoia and insecurity, the bureaucracy as a whole benefited from Stalin's rule. Above all, industry, over which it ruled, grew in size. Its power increased and its position internationally was protected. So although everywhere Stalin was hated, no one could seriously suggest an alternative. Given the goals that the social position of the bureaucracy forced it to accept—building up Russian industry in competition with the West—Stalin's policies and methods seemed inevitable.

While industry continued to expand at an unprecedented rate, many individuals outside the bureaucracy could also benefit. The majority of workers suffered a lowering of living standards, but tens of thousands rose to positions of privilege in the expanding apparatus of control and supervision. At the same time millions moved from the primitive harshness of peasant life to the towns, where if conditions were still miserable, opportunities were greater, horizons wider.

---

* Since the late 1920s (editor's note).

Despite the prophecies of early doom by many of its opponents,[38] the Stalin regime displayed considerable resilience and survived even the crushing military setbacks of the earlier part of the Second World War. Indeed, after the defeat of Germany in 1945, it extended its area of direct control considerably. At the same time it was able to establish regimes in Eastern Europe[39] in many ways identical to the regime in Russia and subordinate to it.

Imperialism and counter-revolution

Stalin's foreign policy flowed from the same motives as his home policy. In the 1930s this implied opposition to revolutionary developments abroad. In the 1940s, 1950s and 1960s there continued to be this hostility; Stalin's lack of support for Mao in China and Tito in Yugoslavia[40] is well documented. Similarly it was pressure from Stalin that made the Italian Communists support the reactionary Badoglio government in Italy at a time when the Socialist and Action Parties both opposed it from the left, and it was Stalin's pressure that made French Communists enter De Gaulle's government in 1944.

But this did not mean, as many of Stalin's leftist opponents believed,[41] that the Russian rulers would not extend their own rule when they got the chance. At the same time as opposing all and every attempt by revolutionaries in the West to topple capitalism, Stalin set about establishing regimes in the areas of Eastern Europe under the direct or indirect control of the Red Army identical to that existing inside Russia. Here Russian influence was used to ensure that Communists obedient to Moscow would be able to use control over the state apparatus—obtained through participation in coalition government with the bourgeois and social democratic parties—to eliminate all other political and social forces, to carry through a 'revolution from above' and to dominate society through a Stalinist apparatus.

In fact there was no contradiction in Stalin's attitude. He was only prepared to support the establishment of Communist regimes where he was convinced that he would be able to control them and where he would not encounter too much hostility in so doing. Such was the case with most of Eastern Europe (and North Korea). A division of the world into Anglo-American and Russian spheres of influence had been decided at the Potsdam and Yalta conferences between Churchill, Roosevelt and Stalin. Although there was jostling at the boundaries (Berlin, Korea) both sides kept to this bargain throughout the post-war period. Stalin did nothing while British and American troops reimposed a reactionary monarchy in Greece by force. The Americans did nothing but make easy propaganda when workers of Berlin and Budapest rose up.

An examination of the economic relations between Russia and the satellites soon reveals the major motivation underlying Russian policy. Control over the states of Eastern Europe was used to subordinate them to the accumulation goals of the Russian bureaucracy. This initially took the form of a more or less crude extraction of booty from these countries. In the case of the countries that had been allied to Germany in the war there were huge 'reparations' (by which those who had first suffered from the policies of reactionary rulers—the ordinary workers and peasants of these countries—were expected to pay for the crimes abroad of their former oppressors). In fact the policy followed was no different to that followed elsewhere, as, for instance, in Manchuria, where the Russian army announced it was seizing industrial equipment as 'war booty.'

The long-term economic development of these countries was subordinated to the demands of Moscow. At the same time the population of these countries was exploited through trade. After 1948 all of them redirected their trade from the West towards Russia. The Russians used a monopoly position to pay less than world market prices for imports from the satellites and to charge more than world prices for their exports to them.[42] One of the major accusations made by the Yugoslavs when they split with the Cominform in 1948 was that Russia's 'revolutionary phraseology conceals counter-revolutionary attempts to prevent industrialisation of our country . . .'[43] The same desire not to be reduced to a mere supplier of cheap raw materials for the rest of Eastern Europe underlay Rumania's breach with Russia in the 1960s. Again, one of the complaints made by the Chinese has been that '. . . the prices of many goods we imported from the Soviet Union were much higher than those on the world market.'[44]

In order to ensure compliance in such policies there was continual purging of the local Communist bureaucracies of Eastern Europe in the early years. Particularly after Tito's break with Stalin, every individual in the leadership of these parties who might conceivably question Russian hegemony was liquidated. In Czechoslovakia the secretary of the Communist Party and ten government ministers were hanged; in Hungary Rajk was executed, Kadar imprisoned and tortured; in Bulgaria Kostov was executed; in Poland Gomulka imprisoned. At the same time thousands of subordinate functionaries and hundreds of thousands of workers also suffered as Russian imperialism tightened its grip.

The failure of monolithism

The Russian and Eastern Europe regimes have been among the most repressive and totalitarian societies in history. Although there were many examples in the pre-capitalist era of societies in which a bureaucracy ruled as a class through its collective control over the state and the major means of production, operating in a coherent fashion to prevent the organisation of any other social force, the utilisation of modern techniques permits systematic repression on an unprecedented scale.

At the same time, however, unlike previous bureaucratic societies, the state capitalist regimes are forced to continually transform the economic basis of their own rule. Their motive force is the continual expansion of the means of production. Inevitably this comes into conflict with the rigid, monolithic and lifeless political structure.

This is most apparent in the international relations of the different Eastern states. As the economies over which they rule change, so the different rulers make differing demands on each other. Each is motivated by the need to build up industry at the fastest possible pace. They will cooperate with the other states only insofar as doing so helps them to achieve that goal. But the moment this is no longer so, cooperation is replaced by violent polemic, mutual condemnation, physical threat and even military conflict. Just as competition between private capitalist states reaches its high point in war, so does competition between so-called 'socialist' state capitalist ones. Thus, once Stalinist regimes independent of Russia were established, the disintegration of the international Communist monolith was inevitable. This in turn made it possible for former Russian satellites like Rumania or North Korea to assert a degree of independence.

But internally as well tensions arise that can tear society apart. For although the state capitalist form of organisation can develop industry at an unprecedented rate under certain conditions, it is not universally successful at doing this.

Oppressive, bureaucratic organisation of production can only succeed in forcing an ever-expanding surplus out of the working population when a more or less complete external control over the actual process of work is possible. But there are production processes that by their very nature are dependent upon the initiative and involvement of the worker.

These cannot be completely controlled from above, if only because no external supervisor can follow every elaborate detail of work.

This has in fact been an element distorting the overall development of the Russian economy from the beginning of the Stalinist era. In agriculture, above all in animal husbandry, the initiative and commitment of the individual worker is central. Bureaucratic methods, far from increasing agricultural production, could actually lead to a decline.

What is true for agriculture is also true for many essential sectors of advanced industrial production. Here too bureaucratic forms of control mean a low level of productivity and poor quality production. This can only be overcome by permitting a devolution of initiative from the central bureaucrats to both local bureaucrats and workers. But these will only respond by improving their output if they feel sufficiently committed to the system to work well without external constraints. So improved productivity demands a raising of living standards and improved working conditions. Failure to provide these can only mean a long-term fall in the rate of accumulation and a weakening of the ability of the bureaucracy to compete internationally.

These problems are aggravated as industrialisation proceeds because previously unemployed resources are used up. In Stalin's time an abundance of resources permitted industrial growth to take place even though these were not efficiently used and labour productivity might be very low. This was no longer possible by the 1950s and 1960s. The result has been a decline in growth rates in all the industrial Stalinist states.

In order to stop this fall in growth rates the bureaucrats have to reorganise their own forms of control over the rest of the population. At the same time they have to transfer resources to sections of the economy producing goods that can raise the living standards of the masses, in other words, to the previously stagnating agricultural and consumer-goods sections.

Compound annual growth rates of national income

	1950–55	1955–60	1960–65
East Germany	11.4	7.0	1.5
Czechoslovakia	8.0	7.1	1.8
USSR	11.3	9.2	6.3
Hungary	6.3	6.5	4.7
Poland	8.6	6.6	5.9
Bulgaria	12.2	9.7	6.5

Two unavoidable problems beset the bureaucracy when it tries to do this:

1. Continued short-term competition with the West (and increasingly with other state capitalist countries) produces strong pressures for a continued high level of investment in heavy industry and arms production. Thus 'owing to the international situation it has not been possible to allocate as many resources as intended to agricultural investment and whilst the 1969 figure exceeds that for 1968 it is below that envisaged in the Directives for 1966–70.'[45] This undercuts the possibility of any long-term improvement in productivity.

2. Any change in the organisation of industry also involves a change in the internal power structure of the bureaucracy itself. Some sections lose out in the process. Among these are the ones most strongly placed to resist such changes: those in charge of the organs of repression, higher managers in heavy industry, among others. Those who exercised power in the past in order to implement the goals of the whole bureaucracy continue to have this power and can now use it to sabotage changes needed to realise production goals under new conditions. They find large numbers of supporters at every level of the state and industrial apparatus. Furthermore, the monolithic organisation of society makes discussion about changes, even within the bureaucracy, difficult. Those who demand changes may well find themselves subject to repression, intimidation, arrest and so on.

So reforms needed to maintain the rate of accumulation cannot be carried through unless there is conscious organisation within the monolithic apparatus to bring them about. Those sections of the apparatus that see the need for reforms have to take counter-measures to protect themselves against powerfully placed conservative bureaucrats.

The classical form under which these processes work themselves out was shown in Hungary and Poland in 1956 and in Czechoslovakia in 1968. In all three cases, those who identified the long-term needs of the bureaucracy as implying reform were unable to overcome conservative resistance by persuasion. Even where formal approval was obtained, reforms were sabotaged in practice. Pressed on by the increasingly urgent economic situation and by fear of what would happen to themselves personally if they lost out, the reformers began to look for allies that would help paralyse their opponents while they themselves took over complete control. At a certain point this meant looking beyond the boundaries of the ruling bureaucracy itself to intermediate groups like students and intellectuals, and even elements among the workers. But in order to gain such support the reforming bureaucrats had to raise slogans expressing the general hostility of society to the police apparatus and Stalinism.

In Poland Gomulka carried this whole manoeuvre through successfully. Once he had taken over the apparatus, he then proceeded to re-establish total bureaucratic control, complete with Stalinist repression.[46]

In Hungary and Czechoslovakia, on the other hand, the attempts by the reformers temporarily to paralyse the repressive apparatus led, although at very different tempos, to the involvement of the mass of the population in the political debate. This in turn led a large section of the reformers, fearing complete popular destruction of their class rule, to change sides at a certain point (in Hungary Kadar, in Czechoslovakia Cernik, Svoboda, and so on). It also produced Russian intervention as the only means capable of ensuring continued bureaucratic control.

At the high points in the bureaucratic in-fighting the 'reformers' in all three cases made seemingly radical, democratic and socialist speeches. Much of the Western press took them at their face value. In fact, however, those who put such slogans forward often came from Stalinist backgrounds, and did not intend in any way to undermine the overall rule of the bureaucracy. They merely wanted to change its particular form. The real significance of what happened in Hungary and Czechoslovakia was not the speeches of Nagy or Dubcek but the fact that the revolution became permanent, moving from bureaucratic to intermediate strata and from these to workers in the factories and streets, culminating in the organisation of workers' councils.

In Russia the chronic crisis of the 1950s and 1960s never became as acute as it did in parts of Eastern Europe. There were bitter power struggles at the top. There were also campaigns aimed at transforming the mode of operation of the whole apparatus (as in the anti-Stalin campaigns of 1956 and 1961–62). But these did not reach the point of completely paralysing the apparatus or of mobilising extra-bureaucratic groups. That was why the Russian state apparatus was able to step into Eastern Europe to redress the balance. At the same time, however, the relative cohesion of the apparatus meant that the fundamental issues at stake in Russia were never confronted. Reforms attempted under Khrushchev were only partially carried through, and in many cases later abandoned.[47]

The experiences of Hungary and Czechoslovakia have demonstrated to the bureaucracy the dangers of division within itself. This, together with the continued immediate pressure of arms competition with the West, strengthens the position of elements opposing wholesale reform. Over the last couple of years* there has been a reversion to a crudely repressive approach to problems. Instead of attempting to come to terms with changes in social forces so as to guarantee its long-term strength, the apparatus tries to freeze them. Reforms are put into effect only half-heartedly and on a tentative basis. Instead there is a crude display of force, externally in relation to Czechoslovakia and China, internally in relation to dissident intellectuals.

But the apparatus as a whole cannot ignore forever its long-term economic problems. The need to come to terms with these continually clashes with the need to reassert cohesion vis-à-vis the rest of society. Instead of having a clear idea of what it is doing and where it is going, the bureaucracy increasingly tries merely to muddle through. Unable to display a clear and determined line of action to the rest of society, its reversion to crude repression will not be enough to frighten dissidents. Despite threats of arrest, imprisonment, loss of livelihood, these continue to make their voices heard in a way impossible under Stalin. No one expects the poets and intellectuals put on trial today to plead guilty and make confessions. At the Moscow trials of the 1930s, despite years of experience in opposing oppressive governments, all the defendants[48] confessed.

The difference arises because today† the bureaucracy is unable to impress even itself that it really knows what it is up to. While increasing the degree of repression, it also behaves in such a way as to increase opposition to repression—so as to necessitate more repression. This in turn makes more difficult the *implementation* of reforms needed to solve its problems. It is trapped in a vicious circle from which there is no way out. The only alternatives are: relative economic stagnation, and therefore increased discontent both within the bureaucracy itself and, more importantly, throughout the population, leading eventually to an elemental explosion of popular forces or a clear split within the bureaucracy, again leading to the self-mobilisation of popular forces.

----

* This refers to the late 1960s (editor's note).
† 1971 (editor's note).

When this occurred in 1956 and 1968 the forces of the state were as affected as the rest of the masses. Only foreign intervention could restore bureaucratic rule. When the eruption hits Moscow and Leningrad, such foreign forces will no longer be available. As the imprisoned Polish revolutionaries Kuron and Modzelewski have written: 'Revolution is a necessity for development. . . . Revolution is inevitable.'[49]

Other interpretations of Russian development

So far we have attempted to account for the degeneration of the Russian revolution and to interpret what has taken place since. It is worth referring briefly here to other interpretations of Russian developments and what follows from them.

Adherents of the most important interpretations still consider Russia to be some form of socialist or workers' state. Insofar as these try to account for the reality of Russian society, they do so by seeing the oppressive features of state policy as flowing from deformations in a basically sound structure. Such interpretations have become increasingly prevalent among leftist and revolutionary circles in the West in recent years.* Since the invasion of Czechoslovakia they have even been popular among various leaders of Western Communist Parties. But the earliest and most far-reaching attempt to carry through such an analysis was that made by Trotsky in the 1930s.[50]

Trotsky argued that the bureaucracy was a foreign body that had grown up in Russia because of the 'contradiction between city and village; between the peasantry and the proletariat; between the national republics and the districts; between the different groups of peasantry; between the different layers of the working class; between the different groups of consumers; and finally between the Soviet state as a whole and its capitalist environment. . . . Raising itself above the toiling masses the bureaucracy regulates these contradictions.'[51] In this way it was able to develop as a 'parasitic caste.' But it was unable to alter the fundamental nature of Russia as a workers' state, said Trotsky. 'The bureaucracy lacks all these social traits [of a class]. It has no independent position in the process of production and distribution.'[52] Rather it had arisen merely to 'regulate inequalities within the sphere of consumption,' to act as a 'gendarme' in the sphere of distribution.

---

* The late 1960s (editor's note).

This meant that the dynamic of development of Russian society could only be seen as resulting from forces other than the bureaucracy. Because it could only survive by balancing between these forces, Stalinism's life span was bound to be very short. 'Bonapartism, by its very essence, cannot long maintain itself: a sphere balanced on the point of a pyramid must invariably roll down on one side or the other.'[53] So the alternatives before the USSR were clear. 'Either the bureaucracy, becoming more and more the organ of the world bourgeoisie within the workers' state, will overthrow the new forms of property and plunge the country back into capitalism or the working class will crush the bureaucracy and open the way to socialism.'[54] And these alternatives would be posed 'within just a few years or even a few months.'

So despite the relative autonomy of its political decision making, for Trotsky the bureaucracy could only register the balance between other forces. It had no independent historical role of its own to play. 'A tumour can grow to a tremendous size and even strangle the living organism, but a tumour can never become a living organism.'[55]

The bureaucracy, however, does display a living dynamic of its own. This was clear even in Trotsky's time. In 1929 the bureaucracy did not just preserve the nationalisation resulting from 1917—it actually nationalised more property through its 'collectivisation' than the revolution had. Nor was this done, as Trotsky depicted it, because the 'Centrists [Stalinists] found their support among the workers . . .'[56] In fact, as we have shown above, the bureaucracy, after years of playing off other social forces one against the other, finally struck out on its own in 1929, hitting at workers and peasants simultaneously.

From that time onwards, attacks on the peasantry did not necessitate concessions to the workers. Nor did attacks on the workers or the few remaining Bolshevik elements in the party necessitate concessions to the peasantry. Failure to see this led to another mistake in Trotsky's analysis—a tendency continually to overestimate the 'strength of bourgeois tendencies within the "socialist" sector itself,'[57] for instance, the 'rich collective farmers.'

Trotsky himself was honest enough to recognise the inadequacies of his own previous analyses as developments incompatible with them took place. But this meant that he was continually being forced to revise both fundamental definitions and conclusions drawn from them. Thus in 1931 he writes that:

The recognition of the present Soviet state as a workers' state not only signifies that the bourgeoisie can conquer power in no other way than by an armed uprising, but also that the proletariat of the USSR has not yet forfeited the possibility of submitting the bureaucracy to it, or of reviving the party again and of mending the regime of the dictatorship—*without a new revolution, with the methods and the road of reform.*[58]

Thus the state is a form of workers' state because the workers can take control of it peacefully.

But by 1935 the reality of conditions in the USSR and of the international policies of the Comintern forced Trotsky to see that only a workers' revolution could reestablish a healthy workers' state. According to his 1931 definition he should have admitted that Russia was no longer any sort of workers' state. Rather than do this he thought it better to change his definition—and incidentally the definition of Marx, Engels and Lenin—of what was a 'workers' state' to one in which what mattered was not actual (or even potential) workers' control over the state, but the fact that property was nationalised. He justified this by arguing that such nationalisation was only possible on the basis of the October revolution. The bureaucracy 'is compelled to defend state property as the source of its power and its income. In this aspect of its activity it still remains a weapon of the proletarian dictatorship.'[59]

When he wrote these words, a decisive argument against the Russian bureaucracy being a new class seemed to Trotsky to be that the 'bureaucracy has not yet created social supports for domination in the form of special types of property.'[60] Yet he was to abandon even this argument, when in one of his last articles[61] he admitted the hypothetical possibility of a ruling class based upon nationalised property.

After the Second World War (and after the murder of Trotsky) developments took place that could not be explained at all within the compass of Trotsky's theory. Firstly, the Russian bureaucracy survived a major historical crisis (the defeats of the Russian armies in the early stages of the war) and emerged, despite all of Trotsky's prophecies, actually strengthened. It extended the physical area of its rule enormously, apparently confounding Trotsky's clear-cut characterisation of its role as 'counter-revolutionary.' Secondly, regimes with characteristics more or less identical to those of Russia were established in several countries without a workers' revolution, without a conscious socialist leadership, and, in several cases, without even the intervention of the Russian 'degenerated workers' state.

Those who continued to adhere to the same interpretation of Russia as Trotsky were then, and have been since, completely at a loss to understand these events. Some have arbitrarily differentiated between different states, calling some 'deformed' or 'degenerated workers' states,' but not the rest. Others have accepted all states with nationalised property as workers' states. In either case, however, what is important is that the line of demarcation is arbitrary. It is not based upon Trotsky's theory but on *ad-hoc* assumptions added in a quite pragmatic and empiricist manner after the event. Above all, in order to avoid an arbitrary distinction between clearly identical regimes in Russia and in the other Eastern states, they are forced to revise a basic element in Marxism: that the establishment of workers' states must be the result of working-class revolution led by a party of conscious militants. In order to defend the form of Trotsky's theory they have to abandon the whole of the Marxist conception to which Trotsky adhered.

The basic fault with all such theories is that they cannot and do not locate the motive forces behind Stalinist policies. They see the body as having a basically socialist metabolism impeded in its operation by warts on it that need erasing, or even by cancers that have to be surgically removed. They do not understand that the very nature of the metabolism has changed. They do not explain what has happened since 1929. They merely record changes afterwards as deviations from a norm. Above all, this inability expresses itself in a failure to understand the international behaviour of the different bureaucratic regimes, the nature of their conflicts with Western imperialism, and the forces that lead them inevitably to conflict and even war with one another.

What is true of Trotsky's theory is true of all other similar theories. By describing Russia and the other bureaucratic states as 'bureaucratised,' 'degenerated,' or 'deformed,' 'socialist' or 'workers' states,' they nowhere locate the forces that determine their development.

What is involved is not just a matter of mistaken definition. Something much more fundamental is at stake. The strength of Marxism as a view of the world lies in the fact that it sees socialism as being possible for the first time in history, so enabling the alienation and exploitation, inhumanity and misery, violence and war that characterise class society to be overcome. The establishment of workers' states is to be the first stage in this process forward. Yet the development of the Eastern states in no way signifies a movement away from alienation, exploitation, misery and war. Experience shows that their policies lead as inevitably to all of these as do those of the ordinary capitalist states. To call such regimes 'socialist' or 'workers' states' is to empty Marxism of its fundamental meaning.

Conclusion

In the past the revolutionary left in the West has continually suffered through its failure to understand that the revolution of 1917 was wiped out by Stalinism years ago. Instead it has shown a false solidarity, has defended the indefensible, has tried to hide from itself realities it could not hide from others. Inevitably this has lowered its ideological credibility, led to disillusion of tens of thousands of its supporters, paralysed it when action was most imperative.

A clear analysis of these regimes is a necessary precondition for renewed growth of the left in the West. Only a theory which centres on the basic problem for the rulers of these countries—that of accumulating capital—and sees this as forcing them into collision with each other and with the working class can comprehend the forms their rule takes and the policies they pursue at each historical point.

This of necessity means recognising the existence of a world system which dominates the ruling classes, both bourgeois and bureaucratic, that sustain it. None of these can behave other than it does without denying the basis for its very existence. None can control the processes that their mutual competition inevitably set into motion. All contribute without hesitation to sustaining forces that in turn compel each to build up industry without reference to human need and to develop monstrous weapons that might destroy humanity for ever. To believe that any one of the ruling classes that participates in this system will be able to end it is absurd. The left hand of Frankenstein's monster can never devour the rest of the body. What is necessary is to organise the real oppositional forces that the system itself breeds. These do exist, on a world scale, as much in the streets of Berlin, Poznan, Budapest or Prague, the factories of Moscow and Leningrad, or the prisons of Siberia as in the paddy fields of Vietnam or the ghettos of the American cities.

FOUR
THE THEORY
OF STATE CAPITALISM
PETER BINNS

EVERYONE who argues for the need for a socialist solution to the problems of our own society has sooner or later to face the question of Russia. This self-proclaimed 'socialist' state has, after all, been responsible for some vile monstrosities: were they 'socialist' slave labour camps in the Gulag Archipelago? Were they 'socialist' tanks that smashed the Hungarian workers' revolt in 1956? Did 'socialist' helicopter gunships strafe villages in Afghanistan in the 1980s? And what about the 'socialist' imprisonment of workers all over Eastern Europe for arguing for free trade unions, most notably today in Poland?

There are two bad answers to these questions.

The first is the most popular. The rulers of Britain, the USSR and the USA—Thatcher, Gorbachev and Reagan—all subscribe to it in one form or another. So too do all too many people on the left. They all agree that Russia really is an example of a socialist society, or is at least on the road to socialism. If they are right, we may as well discard Marxism altogether. Given Russia's faltering growth rate and its continued repression of workers, if this were socialism, then Marxism would have lost all credibility as the theory of the liberation of the masses of ordinary working people.

The second bad answer is to say that Russia, while not being on the road to socialism, is a new form of post-capitalist society. That too

---

First published in *International Socialism*, first series, number 74, in January 1975. It has been updated and revised by the author for publication here.

seriously undermines a socialist strategy at home. For what is there to stop a revolution here going in the same direction? At least here under capitalism workers have the right to organise; shouldn't one then defend a bourgeois democracy against the possibility of a 'post-capitalist' dictatorship, even if the likelihood of it happening is slight? One of the founders of this view, Max Shachtman, ended up supporting American imperialism in Vietnam as a result of following the logic of this argument to its conclusion.

But neither of these is our view. A proper understanding of Russia today, based on Marx's analysis of capitalism, will reveal it to be a form of capitalism itself, *state capitalism*, and neither on the road to socialism nor to an entirely new kind of society. The Russian social system is not different in kind from societies in the West. Russia is an imperialist, capitalist power in just the same way that they are and obeys the same underlying laws of development. It cannot be made socialist by a few reforms here and there, but, as in the West, will require a full-scale workers' revolution against the ruling class and the entire social fabric that preserves their rule.

To see why this is so we must begin by looking at Russia today.

The working class in Russia today

The position of the working class in Russia today is the exact opposite of what it was when it made the 1917 revolution. Then councils—or *soviets*—of workers were the basis of all political power. Today workers are powerless. This is not the place to explain how the revolution was lost—it has been done elsewhere[1]—but the extent of the reversal should be noted.

The income differentials between workers and bosses is every bit as great as the worst the West has to offer in such places as Brazil and the Philippines, and rather greater than in Britain, Germany, Japan and the USA. The spending power of a minister or the president of an academy is at least sixty times the minimum wage paid to office or manual workers.[2] 'Trade unions,' apart from organising holidays, are basically devoted to squeezing more production out of the workers. They are organs of the state which workers are powerless to control. And should workers try to change this they are automatically suppressed. Victor Klebanov is just one of many workers jailed or confined to psychiatric hospital for the crime of arguing for the setting up of genuinely free trade unions.[3] So afraid is the bureaucracy of open discussion that all copying and duplicating facilities are kept under lock and key. The secret police even monitor the whereabouts of every single typewriter in the USSR!

This exploitation and powerlessness of the Russian working class is nothing new. It came about more than fifty years ago. The final vestiges of workers' rights disappeared in 1929 when it was decreed that all managers' orders were now to be 'unconditionally binding on [their] subordinate administrative staff and on all workers.'[4] It was at this time that the trade unions ceased to be able to play any function on behalf of workers, in particular over the negotiation of wages. An internal passport system was introduced, and in 1930 all industrial enterprises were forbidden to employ workers who left their former jobs without permission.[5] Forced or slave labour was introduced on a massive scale as Stalin's terror campaign against the workers gathered momentum in the 1930s. As the Russian authorities themselves cynically put it: 'With the entry of the USSR into the period of socialism, the possibility of using coercive measures by corrective labour have immeasurably increased.'[6]

In Russia the state owns the means of production, but who owns the state? Certainly not the workers! Although its rulers still refer to it as the 'Soviet Union,' the whole idea of a state democratically run by recallable delegates of workers is complete anathema to Gorbachev and company. In fact all efforts to start *any* independent workers' initiatives, let alone workers' councils, are now repressed and standardly rewarded with extreme forms of repression.

From the late 1920s a centralised plan for the economy has been imposed by the leaders on workers and peasants who have had no rights even to object to what has been decided. At the beginning of this process, Kirov—Stalin's second in command at the time—accurately prophesied: 'We shall be pitiless [to] those lacking in firmness in the factories and the villages and who fail to carry out the plan.'[7] Thousands of managers were imprisoned for not repressing their workers enough, and in one incident in 1953 hundreds of slave labourers were shot down for striking over the failure of the authorities to carry out promises of an amnesty.[8] Today the response is more sophisticated—dissident workers who try to set up the most rudimentary forms of workers' defence, such as free trade unions, are now classified as insane and locked up in mental asylums—but the end result is the same.

The periodic elections that take place in Russia are also a complete fraud. For a start all decisions are taken by completely unelected bodies; these are then rubber-stamped by the 'elected' body. Even the highest elected body, the 'Supreme Soviet,' has formal and not real powers. For instance none of the five- and seven-year plans, and none of the sharp turns in foreign policy that marked Stalin's period of office, were even discussed by this supposedly supreme organ of state until after they had already been implemented! Furthermore, 'elections' for this body take place in constituencies where there is *never* more than one candidate standing (nominated from above by the completely undemocratic Communist Party), and where he or she never gets less than 93 per cent of the poll, but sometimes (as with Stalin in 1947) is known to 'receive' as much as 147 per cent![9]

So while the state owns the means of production, it would obviously be complete nonsense to believe that the workers own the state. What kind of society then is Russia? Certainly it is not socialist—the absolute lack of any form of workers' power is clear enough proof of that—but on the other hand it lacks private owners of capital competing with each other as is normally the case in the West. To answer this question therefore, we must first look at capitalism, and in particular at Marx's analysis of its underlying features.

Capitalism and rapidly changing societies

The main reason it is so often assumed that Russia cannot be part of the world capitalist system is because capitalism itself is seen in a certain, rather simplistic way. According to this view it consists of (1) private ownership of the means of production, (2) the regulation of production not by state planning, but by the impersonal 'laws of supply and demand,' and (3) it is assumed that competition between the capitalists takes place only in the marketplace and only through the prices of the commodities sold there. It is then but a short step to define socialism in simple opposition to this, as a society in which there is (1) nationalisation of the means of production, (2) state planning and (3) no free market competition.

Although the society of mid-nineteenth-century Britain, in which Marx wrote *Capital*, came close to this classic picture, this was not at all Marx's own view of the matter. He was well aware, for instance, that capitalism began in England in the seventeenth and eighteenth centuries with looting and slave labour in the colonies as part of its productive base. It also began with trade, but trade based on the vigorous intervention of the state and the denial of anything free about the market at all (the so-called 'mercantilist system').

In discussing the dawn of capitalism Marx stresses not only the growth of the wages system but 'the discovery of gold and silver in America, the extirpation, enslavement and entombment in mines of the aboriginal population, the beginning of the conquest and looting of the East Indies, the turning of Africa into the warren for the commercial hunting of black skins, signalised the rosy dawn of the era of capitalist production . . . Great fortunes sprang up like mushrooms in a day: primitive accumulation went on without the advance of a shilling.'[10] And instead of the 'invisible hand' of the laws of supply and demand, in Britain there was 'a systematic combination, embracing the colonies, the national debt, the modern mode of taxation, and the protectionist system. These methods depend in part on brute force, e.g., the colonial system. But they all employ the power of the state.'[11]

That is why Marx warns us: 'If, then, the specific form of capital is abstracted away, and only the content is emphasised . . . Capital is conceived as a thing, not as a relation . . . [but] capital is not a simple relation but a *process*, in whose various moments it is always capital.'[12] Because it is a process, and one which contains contradictions, it is always changing itself as it develops. We need to understand its *dynamic*—the underlying principle according to which it changes and develops.

Capitalism remains capitalism throughout its various changes because its central dynamic, its internal motor, remains unchanged, and it is to this that we now turn.

Accumulation: The key to capitalism's development

The thing which links the early stage of capitalist development, based on monopoly, looting and slavery, with later stages like those of nineteenth-century private capitalism and twentieth-century state capitalism, is the nature of the accumulation process. In all of these stages the direct producers are exploited, and the fruits of this exploitation—Marx called it 'surplus value'—is *accumulated* in further means of production. This is quite unlike what happened in pre-capitalist societies, such as feudalism and the Ancient World, where exploitation led not to accumulation but rather to the ruling class consuming in more and more opulent ways.

In *The Communist Manifesto* Marx neatly summarises this point and contrasts the capitalist and socialist modes of production. In the former:

> . . . the labourer lives merely to increase capital, and is allowed to live only in so far as the interest of the ruling class requires it. In bourgeois society, living labour is but a means to increase accumulated labour. In Communist society, accumulated labour is but a means to enrich, to widen, to promote the existence of the labourer. In bourgeois society, therefore, the past dominates the present; in Communist society the present dominates the past. [13]

The crucial thing about capitalism is that it is a society in which, firstly, the exploited creative energy of the working class becomes piled-up in an ever-expanding quantity of productive forces, and, secondly, the past history of this accumulation is the central determinant of what is happening *now* in capitalist society.

In *Capital Marx* develops this point more fully. He stresses that the motive force of capitalism is not the consumption of the capitalist, but the fact that in order to fulfil his role as a capitalist at all he has to accumulate:

> [The capitalists'] own private consumption is a robbery perpetrated on accumulation . . . Accumulate, accumulate! That is Moses and the prophets! . . . Therefore, save, save, i.e. reconvert the greatest possible portion of surplus value, or surplus product, into capital! Accumulation for accumulation's sake, production for production's sake . . . What then makes this drive to accumulation—and the subordination of the whole of society to it—possible in the first place? Two factors are needed; together they give us a society fully ruled by the laws of capitalism. [14]

Firstly the working class must be forcibly separated from the ownership and control of the means of production. This is crucial; without it workers would never consent to their own exploitation. If workers controlled production as a whole, it would be subordinated to fulfilling workers' needs—in other words to use, to consumption. They might of course freely decide to set aside a portion of production to expand future production, but this would be a different matter altogether—it would only be a *means* to the further end of consumption, workers would rule accumulation rather than being ruled by it.

Secondly there has to be competition between those who own the means of production. Without it each capitalist could freely decide whether to consume the fruits of the exploitation of the working class, to accumulate it, or even to return it to the workers who created it. What makes the system into a capitalist one is the fact that he is compelled to accumulate it. The compulsion comes from the process of competition, which threatens each capitalist with extinction by rival capitalists if he doesn't invest in the most modern and efficient equipment—and hence accumulate capital. That is why, as Marx put it, 'competition makes the immanent laws of capitalist production to be felt by each capitalist, as external coercive laws.'[15]

Competition: The mainspring of capitalism

Competition then, is the mainspring of capitalism. It drives on the process of the accumulation of capital. For Marx is it 'nothing other than the inner nature of capital, appearing in and realised as the reciprocal interaction of many capitals with one another.'[16]

But while it drives on the accumulation process, the accumulation process itself reacts back on it, and in doing so can transform the mechanisms of competition in crucial ways. Even though Marx was writing *Capital* at the high point of classic 'laissez-faire' capitalism, he was well aware of this in general terms. He knew, for instance, as we have already mentioned, that the capital accumulation process in the seventeenth and eighteenth centuries led not to less but to more state involvement in the marketplace. He also knew that this involved a strengthening of *military* competition between the newly emerging capitalist states.

Marx recognised that the *form* of competition is continuously changed by the accumulation process. This was not just something confined to capitalism's infancy but had immediate implications for the capitalism of his own day as well. Crisis, he argued, was endemic to capitalism, and it led not only to the increase in the size of the capitals which confront each other as a result of accumulation but also to a *reduction in the numbers* of independent units of capital that remain to confront each other.[17] In a period of crisis, some companies would be forced out of business— their accumulations of capital (factories, goods, machinery and so on) being taken over by other, even larger, capitalists. Competition thus leads to the concentration and the *centralisation* of capital. Marx remarked:

> Today, therefore, the force of attraction, drawing together individual capitals, and the tendency to centralisation are stronger than ever before . . .
> In any given branch of industry centralisation would reach its extreme limit if all the individual capitals invested in it were fused into a single

capital. In a given society the limit would be reached only when the entire social capital was united in the hands of either a single capitalist or a single capitalist company.[18]

In Marx's own lifetime the most important channel for the centralisation of capital was not the merger or the takeover bid but the conversion of an individual's capital into his part-ownership of a joint-stock company. Of this process Marx said:

> This is the abolition of the capitalist mode of production within the capitalist mode of production itself, and hence a self-dissolving contradiction, which *prime facie* represents a mere phase of transition to a new form of production. It manifests itself as such a contradiction in its effects. It establishes a monopoly in certain spheres and thereby requires state interference. It reproduces a new financial aristocracy, a new variety of parasites in the shape of promoters, speculators and simply nominal directors; a whole system of swindling and cheating by means of corporation promotion, stock issuance and stock speculation. It is private production without the control of private property.[19]

Updating this passage to the 1890s, Engels commented:

> Since Marx wrote the above, new forms of industrial enterprise have developed . . . the old boasted freedom of competition has reached the end of its tether and must itself announce its obvious, scandalous bankruptcy . . . in some branches . . . competition has been replaced by monopoly.[20]

Arguing against socialists in Germany who wanted to simply identify capitalism with private production, Engels, in his 'Critique of the Erfurt Programme,' writes:

> I know of capitalist production as a social form, as an economic stage; and of capitalist *private* production as a phenomenon occurring one way or another within that stage. What does capitalist *private* production mean then? Production by a single entrepreneur, and that is of course becoming more and more an exception. Capitalist production through *limited companies* is already no longer private production, but production for the combined account of many people. And when we move on to the Trusts, which control and monopolise whole branches [of industry], then that means an end not only to the *private production*, but also to the planlessness.[21]

Marx and Engels, then, are very clear on a number of points. Firstly the capitalist production process produces—and will inevitably go on producing—fewer, but much bigger, concentrations of capital. Secondly, this implies that, as the capitalist system ages, the 'invisible hand' of the laws of supply and demand posited by Adam Smith no longer suffices to regulate the economy. Marx talks about production under these circumstances as being 'without the control of private production,' and he argues that it 'requires state interference.' For Engels 'the old boasted freedom of competition has reached the end of its tether' and 'that means an end . . . to . . . private production.'

Finally, and crucially, both Marx and Engels are very clear that under these circumstances we do *not* have a new, post-capitalist mode of production. Certainly Marx talks of it as 'the abolition of the capitalist mode of production,' but then immediately adds '*within the capitalist mode of production itself*,' as if to say that it *appears* to be a move away from the capitalist mode of production when looked at in isolation, but is really an intrinsic part of it when seen in the context of the dynamic of the system as a whole. And Engels has no hesitation at all in dismissing the view that capitalist production can only take place under conditions of 'private production' and 'planlessness.'

The rapid rise in the role of the state in the Western capitalist economies in the twentieth century confirms Marx and Engels' analysis on this point. By the 1960s in Italy the state was responsible for the majority of fixed capital formation; in Bangladesh in the 1970s the state held 85 per cent of the assets of what it termed 'modern industrial enterprise'; in Algeria it was employing 51 per cent of all workers in industry, construction and trade in 1972; in Turkey it was responsible for 40 per cent of value added in industry in 1964; in Brazil for well over 60 per cent of all investment by the mid-1970s; and in Britain for 45 per cent of fixed capital formation in the same period.[22]

But this immediately raises a further question. If planlessness and private production is but one stage in the development of capitalism, and yet competition remains capitalism's 'inner essence,' what form can competition take which is not tied to this private form of property but which can still regulate production and cause the dynamic of capitalist development to continue?

Aging capitalism in the West

As we have seen, at the end of the golden age of nineteenth-century private production, Engels was writing of 'private production' and 'planlessness' as but one 'stage' of capitalism's development, yet at no point did he even question that competition is capitalism's 'inner essence.' Clearly implicit in this is the understanding that competition must be able to take on forms other than that of price competition between commodities produced by private capitals for an autonomous market.

Such considerations as these formed the starting point for the most fruitful developments of Marxist theory at the beginning of this century. Grappling with the rapid drive of the system to imperialism and world war, Lenin, Bukharin and others, basing their ideas on these premises, began to argue that 'peaceful' competition was more and more turning into a variety of more violent forms—the physical seizure of colonies and raw materials, the exclusion of rival capitalists by the erection of tariff walls, and above all the threat, or the actual use of direct military power itself.

For Bukharin (supported by Lenin)[23] this is due to two main consequences of capitalist crisis, as explained by Marx's theory. Firstly, within each country economic power was becoming concentrated and centralised into the hands of fewer and fewer giant corporations. Secondly, in order to exploit the efficiencies implicit in a world division of labour, each capital was becoming impelled to extend its tentacles beyond its own national borders.

The first tendency implies a greater and greater integration of the corporation with the state; the second implies an extension of its operations overseas. The combination of the two necessarily leads to the national state bursting through its purely geographical borders, and in the long run to the collision of one state's external tentacles with those of another.

But there is a difference between this and the situation where one purely private capital confronts another. When one state or state-backed corporation collides with another, this implies that the sharper the conflict the more it will take on a directly military form, and the more the corporations will take on the form of what Bukharin called 'state capitalist trusts':

> When competition has reached its highest stage . . . then the use of state power, and possibilities connected with it, begin to play a very large part . . .

[But] even if free competition were entirely eliminated within the boundaries of 'national economies,' crises would still continue, as there would remain the anarchic structure of world economy . . . This anarchic structure of world capitalism is expressed in two facts: world industrial crises on the one hand, wars on the other . . .

The struggle between state capitalist trusts is decided in the first place by the relation between their military forces, for the military power of the country is the last resort of the struggling 'national' groups of capitalists.[24]

It follows from this analysis that two tendencies are simultaneously and mutually implicit in aging capitalism: the first is the growing together of capital and the state, and the second is the tendency for war between the various, increasingly statised, capitals. *The two are not at all separate, the one mutually implies the other.*

It is important to stress this point. If you accept that aging capitalism implies imperialism and war along the lines that the classical Marxists argued, the corollary is that this involves—and must involve—the increasing statisation of capital, and that the more any national capital or group of capitals is statised the more its mutual competition with other capitals will take the form of direct military competition.

In short, long before the processes which gave rise to Stalin's rule in Russia had occurred, the world economy had already moved decisively into a new epoch. It is true that many barriers existed which prevented these tendencies referred to by Lenin and Bukharin from being at all fully implemented at the time in the West. Still others were partially (though only partially) dismantled for a temporary period of time in the 1920s. For all that, the central point remains: the world which surrounded Russia after Stalin rose to power out of the ashes of the 1917 revolution was one which was pressurising all the component states in the system to play a more central role in the economy than ever before. When Stalin and the Russian bureaucracy moved so decisively in this direction themselves in 1928 therefore, it was not at all against the trend of world capitalism. On the contrary it fitted it like a hand fits a glove.

Russia considered in isolation from the rest of the world

How then does the Russian economy and state appear today in this context? Two features, as we saw earlier, were necessary for the specifically capitalist tendency of accumulation for the sake of accumulation:

(1) separation of the workers from the means of production, and (2) competition between the capitalists.

Obviously the first of these exists in an extreme form in Russia. It is more developed than in the West due to the increased powers of repression of a totalitarian police state.

But what about the second feature? Overwhelmingly it is the case that *within* the Russian economy there is centralised administration of production. Individual productive units have rarely been autonomous or in competition with each other. In Western capitalism we are used to the attempt to plan and cooperate within any given enterprise, coupled with competition outside it. Russia, *considered purely on its own*, lacks the mechanisms for introducing this competitive element. As Tony Cliff puts it: 'The division of labour within Russian society is in essence a species of the division of labour within a single workshop.'[25]

If any one capitalist enterprise, General Motors or IBM, say, had successfully managed to take over the whole of the world economy, capitalism would have ceased to exist. Competition between capitals would end, and therefore so too would accumulation for the sake of accumulation and production for the sake of accumulation. This would not be socialism, of course, but a new class society—one which Bukharin characterised as an industrial 'slave-owning economy where the slave market is absent.'[26]

This gives us an accurate picture of what Russia might have been like had it been possible to remain in isolation from the rest of the world— just like this but on a smaller scale.

What this means is that *if Russia were unaffected by the world around it*, it could no longer be a society explicable by the laws of capitalism. Enterprises in Russia would not be forced by mutual competition to accumulate. The purpose of production would be the creation of use values rather than the revenue obtained from selling them. Russia would have become a gigantic corporation in which the state had become the repository for all the means of production. In these two respects, state ownership of the means of production, and use values as the purpose of production, *and in these respects alone*, it would resemble a workers' state. It would also resemble Egypt of the pharoahs and the ancient civilisations of Assyria and the Indus Valley, not just in these two respects, but also as a hierarchical class society in which the producers themselves did not control production.

The beginning of state capitalism in Russia

But of course Russia never could have been isolated from the rest of the world. Lenin was an internationalist not just because he *wanted* world socialism, but because he knew that the only way to get socialism anywhere, including Russia, was for the working class to seize power in the dominant industrial capitalist countries:

> We always staked our play upon an international revolution and this was unconditionally right . . . We always emphasised . . . the fact that in one country it is impossible to accomplish such a work as a socialist revolution.[27]

Again, in March 1919, Lenin repeated:

> We do not live merely in a state but in a system of states and the existence of the Soviet Republic side by side with imperialist states for any length of time is inconceivable. In the end one or the other must triumph.[28]

Lenin made it clear that the source of this incompatibility was not just the military intervention of the imperialist powers against Russia after the revolution, but Russia's economic dependence upon the surrounding capitalist states; for he refers to the '. . . international market to which we are subordinated, with which we are connected and from which we cannot escape.'[29]

The extreme backwardness of Russia in an age of imperialism forced it to industrialise rapidly. If the revolutions in Germany and elsewhere had succeeded, plenty of means of production and skilled labour could have flowed into Russia to accomplish this task. But when the perspective changed from stressing the need to spread the revolution internationally to stressing the building of 'socialism' in a single country, as proposed by Stalin in 1924, the situation was completely reversed. If industrialisation was to take place in Russia *in isolation* it could only be by extracting huge surpluses from the working class, and by forcing many peasants off the land into the mines and the steel mills.

The new ruling bureaucracy could only retain power insofar as it could succeed in this task. It required a vast terror apparatus to subordinate the consumption of the masses to the accumulation needs of the Russian state. For a time Stalin tried to avoid this logic. He allied with the right wing in the Bolshevik Party, which spoke of 'proceeding towards social-ism at a snail's pace' without attacks on the peasantry. But this meant that what accumulation there was in the years 1923–28 went into the social services, education, agriculture and food, rather than heavy industry. Very little progress was made in these years towards catching up with the West.

An increase in international tension in 1927 showed the danger of the policy: without a more rapid rate of accumulation there was no way (other than international revolution, already ruled out by Stalin) of defending Russia. Stalin was forced to change tack and follow a policy which went for all-out accumulation, regardless of the interests of Russian workers or, for that matter, individual bureaucrats.

The state was thus cut loose from its original social base. Having become heavily bureaucratised it moved decisively to take upon itself the role of massive capital accumulation in the first five-year plan of 1928–33. It did so because of the increasing pressure from world imperialism. As Stalin put it in 1931:

> No comrades . . . the pace must not be slackened! . . . On the contrary we must quicken it as much as is within our powers and possibilities . . . To slacken the pace would be to lag behind; and those who lag behind are beaten . . . We are fifty or a hundred years behind the advanced countries. We must make good this lag in ten years. Either we do it or they crush us.[30]

The last vestiges of workers' control were eliminated from the factories. Real wages were slashed and a general speed-up was introduced. Peasants were forcibly driven off the land to become factory fodder in the cities. The bureaucracy thus began a massive, primitive accumulation of capital. The results were immediate. Investment in industry expanded six times its 1923–28 level in the years 1928–33, and thereafter doubled in each of the succeeding five-year periods.[31]

The imposition of capitalist relations of production

In Russia, the subordination of consumption to the needs of accumulation took on an extreme form. From the beginning of the first five-year plan capital accumulation absorbed more than 20 per cent of the national income, and it increased in subsequent plans.[32] This was higher than any of the developed capitalist countries outside Russia (but about the same as the USA and Japan in their equivalent periods of development), and shows clearly that this most characteristic symptom of capitalism—the domination of society by capital accumulation—was fully developed in Russia at that time.

Accumulation and not consumption thus became the goal of production in Russia. Acting as the agent for the accumulation of capital, the bureaucracy emerged as the collective capitalist at the same pace as the economy itself took on the same features of the giant corporations in the nations of the West against which Russia was competing.

The bureaucracy's monopoly of foreign trade enabled it to seal off Russia from *price* competition. But *strategic* and *military* competition completely dominated the process of capital formation in Russia from the moment accumulation became the bureaucracy's central concern in 1928. From the beginning of the five-year plans armaments dominated the accumulation process. For instance in machine-building plants, which are probably the best gauge of the development of accumulation, already by 1932 munitions plants accounted for as much as 46 per cent of total iron and steel consumed. By 1938 this figure had risen to the staggering sum of 94 per cent,[33] and virtually all other machinery plant construction had ceased!

Accumulation in the period before the Second World War was dominated by strategic and military competition with the Western nations. This was even more true for Russia after the war. Between 1950 and 1965 approximately *twice as large a percentage* of the national income was spent on armaments as in the 1930s, even though the proportion of total income accumulated throughout the economy remained largely unchanged.[34] The effect this had was for armaments to be directly responsible for around two-thirds of all capital accumulated in this period.[35]

Since 1928, therefore, not only has consumption been subordinated to accumulation, but in addition we can find the reasons for this in the competitive, coercive structure of world capitalism—which accounts for the vast bulk of Russia's tendency for accumulation for the sake of accumulation. It is not their own desires therefore, but the logic of world capitalism which forces the bureaucracy to accumulate.

The dynamic of Russian society determined by the world around it

Basically Russia is like one big factory, and although *if* it had existed in a vacuum the laws of capitalist development would cease to apply to it, that is obviously not the present case. Its actual behaviour is therefore based upon the same laws which govern the actions of other corporations. Of course we know that when corporations get very big and are drawn closer together with the state, we have to modify these laws. But the modifications are always *on the basis of the original laws*, and because of this they always preserve the basic tendencies and contradictions even if in a distorted form.

All this is another way of saying what we remarked upon at the beginning—that capitalism is a process in continuous movement, not an unchanging thing. We identify it by its inherent tendencies, by its *dynamic*. That is why we look to Russia's accumulation for accumulation's sake, based upon competition with Western capitalism, as the key to explaining changes in its internal structure rather than the other way about.

Marx himself argues in just the same way when he analyses the economy of the plantation slave states in America in the 1850s.

If we look purely at the *internal* workings of the plantations there is a simple conclusion to be drawn. There is no internal labour market on the plantation and the slave-owners do not purchase labour power within it. Elsewhere Marx had argued that for capitalism to exist it had to be the case 'that the owner of the labour-power should sell it only for a definite period, for if he were to sell it rump and stump, once for all, he would be selling himself, converting himself from a free man into a slave, from an owner of a commodity into a commodity. He must constantly look upon his labour power as his own property, his own commodity, and this he can only do by placing it at the disposal of the buyer temporarily, for a definite period of time. By this means alone can he avoid renouncing his rights of ownership over it.'[36] It follows from this that, looked at purely on their own, the plantation slave states were not capitalist.

Yet looked at as a whole and considering their links with the rest of the world, Marx has no doubts: '. . . we now not only call the plantation owners in America capitalists,' he tells us, 'but . . . they *are* capitalists.'[37] This is because 'Negro slavery *presupposes* wage labour, and if other, free states with wage labour did not exist alongside it, if, instead, the Negro states were isolated, then all social conditions there would immediately turn into pre-civilised forms.'[38]

Marx's methodology is very clear here. Looked at purely on their own the slave states lack an essential aspect of capitalism. But within the context of a coercive world economy the position changes. On the surface there is no free wage-labour, but because the plantation owners have to compete, for instance, with cotton-producing landlords from Egypt in the British market, they are compelled to exploit their slaves to a certain degree, to mechanise and so on. External competition therefore, and external competition alone, enforces on the plantations a capitalist dynamic, and on the slaves a need to produce surplus value for the owners.

For Marx there was never any question of looking for a completely separate set of laws to explain the economy of the Southern slave states; it was sufficient to show that—notwithstanding the fact that the plantation owner has not hired labour power but, rather, has bought the direct producer 'rump and stump'—the plantations were forced to act as any other unit of capital would because of external coercion from rival capitalists.

Exactly the same methodology reveals the capitalist nature of the bureaucracy in Russia. Of course Russian workers are not slaves; they are paid in roubles; they have some choice over which enterprise they work in and they can use their wages to purchase—within limits—the commodities of their choice. Nonetheless, if 'Russia Inc.' is in essence one single enterprise, then for all intents and purposes from birth to death the state bears all the costs of the upkeep of its workers and in turn reaps all the benefits from their labouring activities. In this respect the plantation owner and the Russian bureaucracy are in comparable positions. What makes Russia part of the capitalist world system is not the fact that workers are paid wages or can move from one state sector to another, but rather the fact that the Russian bureaucracy is forced to exploit them to a certain degree, to modernise the plant and equipment they work with, to accumulate capital, to distribute the workers from one sector to another, and it is forced to do these things, in the direction and to the extent that it is, solely because of the competitive pressure of the world around it.

Use values and exchange values in Russia and the West

The difference between the Southern slave owners and the bureaucracy in Russia today is, of course, that the former sold the great bulk of their production on the world market, whereas foreign trade accounts for only a small fraction of total production in Russia (and the amount that is traded outside the Comecon area is even smaller, less than a twentieth of total production).

This combination of a centrally administered internal economy plus a low level of foreign trade has led many people to argue that Russia is not really part of the capitalist world. They argue that Russia cannot be capitalist because the internal organisation of the economy is not based upon competition of goods on the market. Firms produce according to instructions laid down by a central authority. It is said that therefore, by definition, these firms cannot be turning out *commodities* and Russia cannot be capitalist.

Marx says that the production of goods which are not exchanged with other goods on the market is the production of *use-values*, not *exchange-values*: 'To become a commodity a product must be transferred to another, to whom it will serve as a use-value, by means of an exchange.'[39] Therefore, it is argued, Russia cannot be capitalist.

How are we to assess these arguments?

To begin with, we should note that an important reason why external trade plays so small a role in Russia is that it is such a big country. Like the USA, its proportion of foreign trade to total production is much less than with smaller countries. East Germany, for instance—with a socio-economic structure more or less identical with that of Russia—trades a much higher proportion of its total production than either the USA or Russia.

Also we should note that if this argument were correct, then much of production in the West could not be capitalist either. We have mentioned already the large state sectors of the Western economies that flourished from the 1940s to the 1970s, but on top of that there has been the substantial chunk of 'private' industry that has produced only for the state—highway construction and armaments firms for instance. And during the period of total war 1940–1945, state control of wages, prices, what was produced, how much, and by whom became far more total in Britain and Germany—archetypal Western capitalist nations—than is the norm in the economies of the Eastern bloc countries today.

Furthermore the non-state sector in the West is increasingly dominated by giant corporations: in Britain today a hundred firms, dominated by interlocking directorships, control half the private sector production.

Within both the state sector and the giant corporations, the individual productive units do not in the main produce for the market, but instead for other sections of the same enterprise, according to instructions laid down in advance. A single plant may well produce goods not for exchange, but for use by other plants inside the same combine. Yet in the long run, all the different stages of production within the factory tend to obey the laws of capitalism.

The individual capitalist is under pressure to impose the laws of capitalism within his own factory, even though there is planning within the factory, in order to maximise his profit. Although workers in one part of the factory are producing use values for workers in other parts of the factory—not exchange values—their production is regulated by similar considerations as if they were producing commodities for the market. The external relations between the factory and the rest of the economy transform the different stages of production within the factory into stages of capitalist production.

The same considerations apply when we look at the operation of the giant corporations. Although vast areas of their operations are planned and very remote from the market, in the last analysis their competition with other corporations ensures that capitalist laws prevail.

Production for the military needs of the state is not qualitatively different from this. Although the goods involved are never going to be exchanged on a competitive market (in Britain only 10 per cent of arms are sold to anyone but the British government), those who plan production are still compelled to impose the laws of capitalism on it. Normally they do this by using various devices to compare the performance, costing and so on in the arms sector with other sectors. On the basis of such measurements, the state agrees to the arms barons receiving a certain level of remuneration.

So although the arms companies rarely compete for markets with anyone, they have to behave as if they do. Capitalism continues to exist—even though the state bureaucracy acts as a *substitute* for the market.

In each case the mechanisms that are employed internally are similar. Labour has to be exploited as efficiently as by the rival; productivity has continually to be jacked up. Although the individual firm or country may plan its operations, the content of this 'plan' depends on its relationship to its rival: if it cannot match its rival's increases in the rate of exploitation or advances in technology, then it will be in danger. What determines the internal organisation of each country, as of each firm, is its relationship to a total system outside itself.

That is why the huge arms sector of the US economy today is a capitalist sector: it has to compare its productivity, its level of technology and its labour costs with those of the rest of the Western countries and with the Russian economy, because of economic competition with Europe and Japan and military competition with Russia.

Similarly for the Russian economy as a whole. If it is dominated by arms production (as we have shown above) then it is dominated by its relationship with production outside Russia. What matters to the rulers of Russia is not how many use values they pile up in the abstract, but how these use values compare with the use values piled up by the American arms economy.

But when two piles of use values are measured up against one another, they cease to be merely use values. They begin to behave as exchange values: their value no longer depends upon their intrinsic qualities, but upon their relationship to production throughout the world system.

The very things which the rulers of Russia worry about show how they are dominated in all their calculations by such considerations just as much as any Western corporation. When they talk about rates of growth, it is rates of growth compared with the West. They are not worried about the outputs of labour as such, but labour productivity compared with the West. They are obsessed with their low rate of innovation, again, compared with the West.

The key areas of economic decision-making which affect workers are made according to the same sorts of calculations that apply in the West: how can the profitability of different sectors be improved? How can workers be persuaded to accept a cut in the labour force and increased output in return for more pay? What level of wages is needed to ensure that workers produce at the greatest possible speed? The consequences of the competitive relationship with the West are inescapable.

Marx moves from an analysis of individual commodity production at the beginning of volume 1 of *Capital* to the dynamic of capitalism, accumulation, towards the end. This article began by showing that in Russia, as in the West, everything is subordinated to accumulation. Now we can see that accumulation is in turn the result of the competitive relationship between the Russian ruling class and its rivals, which transforms the output of Russian industry as a whole into production dominated by the essentially capitalist criterion of exchange value.

The contradictions of state capitalism

If Russia is economically speaking just like one huge corporation, then the familiar contradictions of capitalism must appear there too. That means that sooner or later the rate of profit must fall.

In the West this has in the past signalled the beginning of a slump. Investment ceases, demand declines, overproduction begins, and then capital values collapse. Out of the crisis the weakest units of capital become bankrupt and are absorbed at bargain prices by the stronger units of capital. This restructures capital and makes it possible for it to function again. With rivals bankrupt and capital values much lower, the rate of profit temporarily recovers and the cycle begins anew.

But in Russia there is no such mechanism connecting overproduction with the restructuring of capital. Major investment decisions are centrally administered, and there is no means whereby the bureaucrat who makes the decisions will change them automatically. For the factory manager too, it is a matter of indifference whether his goods get consumed or remain untouched in a warehouse, or whether his new factory premises are completed or left unfinished. This is hardly a sign that the Russian economy is crisis free—exactly the opposite is the case; it is a clear indication that the economy is in a state of *permanent* crisis. Western capitalism has mechanisms of a greater or a lesser efficiency for restructuring capital in crisis, but Russia has no such internal means of doing so. So further accumulation at this point actually does continue, but it fails to expand the sum total of use values in the economy. It has reached a state of permanent stagnation.

Only comparatively recently has this become of crucial importance. Until the 1950s underutilised labour was so freely available that primitive accumulation could proceed and absorb new investment profitably. Until then Russia could continue to devote its principal accumulation resources to expanding the means of production. But because all means of production must, after an initial lag, contribute to the means of consumption, this merely delayed the crisis. It cannot stop the state of permanent stagnation occurring, but only delay the time when it appears.

The return of the world capitalist system to crisis in the 1970s did not leave the Eastern state capitalist economies untouched. The evidence here is irrefutable. It can be seen in declining growth rates, falling rates of profit, marked cyclical tendencies, an increasing technology gap, and huge balance of payments deficits which have required vast borrowing on the international finance market. The effects of this crisis on the Eastern bloc economies have been very serious indeed.

Firstly, even before the crises of 1974 and 1980, there was a marked and continuous decline in growth rates not only in Russia but in all the Eastern European state capitalist economies.

Only Poland was able to stave off crisis in this period—but at the cost of suffering more than any other major capitalist nation, East or West, in the crises of 1974 and especially 1980. Poland kept up its growth by a massive increase in trade with the West, which was itself undergoing a short but very rapid boom from 1971–1973. Imports from the West *tripled* from 1970 to 1973, and by 1975 only 45 per cent of Poland's trade was with all the other Eastern bloc countries put together. Then came the slump. Poland's exports plummeted, and the cost of the imports needed to maintain growth soared.

Rates of growth (percentages)

	1950–55	1955–60	1960–65	1965–70
USSR	11.3	9.2	6.3	4.0
Czechoslovakia	8.0	7.1	1.8	3.4
Poland	8.6	6.6	5.9	6.7
Bulgaria	12.2	9.7	6.5	4.5

Having participated in the world boom, the Polish bureaucracy was hit by the inflationary pressures it created. By 1975 Eastern Europe's net borrowing from the West rocketed to $20 billion, of which Poland's share was the then incredible sum of $7 billion.[41] Servicing this debt took a quarter of all its foreign earnings.

The process was repeated in a much more extreme way in the 1980 crisis. But this time servicing the new debt of over $20 billion took more than 90 per cent of Poland's foreign earnings and there was a massive fall in production of at least 15 per cent in 1981.[42]

Until recently the USSR, however, still had a surplus rural population, and hence from 1950 to 1970 it was able to expand the urban labour force by around 4 per cent per year. Even with stagnant labour productivity it was therefore guaranteed a minimum growth rate of 4 per cent. But today the urban labour force is growing at less than 1 per cent per year and it has therefore become crucial to expand productivity.[43]

The urgency is revealed by the fact that today the Eastern European economies have growth rates that are broadly similar to those of the Western countries (somewhat better than Britain and somewhat worse than Japan), but that they are only able to achieve this on the basis of *twice the level of investment*.[44] This would suggest, then, a rough-and-ready figure for the rate of profit at about 50 per cent of that prevailing in the West.

Russia today is more than ever dependent on wheat from the Americas and high technology engineering from Europe and Japan. It is quite beyond its own technological and financial resources to launch many of its most important investments without partnerships with the West. The Russian state capitalist ruling class is therefore constrained by just the same forces as those applying in the West, while more and more its own activities contribute to—and suffer from—the rhythm of the world market.

As in the West, socialism can be achieved in Russia only through a workers' revolution that totally destroys the power of the ruling class and replaces it with workers' power from below—and on an international basis. There can be no half-way measures or fudged compromises. Gorbachev's Russia is not even a partially 'progressive' formation, and its ruling class is as much a barrier to socialism for Russian workers as are the ruling classes in the West for Western workers.

EIGHTY YEARS SINCE
THE RUSSIAN REVOLUTION

AHMED SHAWKI

The Russian Revolution of October 1917 remains to this day the most decisive event of the international workers' movement. The Russian events took place in the midst of the barbaric carnage known as World War I. The swift overthrow of the tsar in February of that year and the almost bloodless Bolshevik-led insurrection in October held out the hope for millions across Europe.

The Bolshevik revolution was by no means a specifically 'Russian' phenomenon. As Lenin was later to put it, Bolshevism had become "world Bolshevism" by virtue of its revolutionary tactics, theory and program. By indicating the "right road of escape from the horrors of war and imperialism . . . Bolshevism *can serve as a model of tactics for all.*"[1]

The significance of the revolution was not lost on ruling classes and politicians around the world, especially in Europe. Fear that the revolution would spread gripped the bourgeoisie. Not a friend of revolutionary socialism, British prime minister Lloyd George wrote,

> The whole of Europe is filled with the spirit of revolution. There is a deep sense not only of discontent but of anger and revolt amongst the workmen against the pre-war conditions. The whole existing order in its political, social and economic aspects is questioned by the masses of the population from one end of Europe to the other.[2]

The prospects of revolution which produced paroxysms of fear in the rich were eagerly welcomed by socialists. Victor Serge wrote:

The newspapers of the period are astonishing . . . riots in Paris, riots in Lyon, revolution in Belgium, revolution in Constantinople, victory of the soviets in Bulgaria, rioting in Copenhagen. In fact the whole of Europe is in movement, clandestine or open soviets are appearing everywhere, even in the Allied armies; everything is possible, everything.[3]

Antiwar socialist and journalist John Reed cabled the *New York Call* with news of the Bolshevik victory. Under the headline, "John Reed Cables the *Call* News of the Bolshevik Revolt He Witnessed," the sub-head read: "First Proletarian Republic Greets American Workers." Reed began his article with characteristic bluntness:

This is the revolution, the class struggle, with the proletariat, the soldiers and peasants lined up against the bourgeoisie. Last February was only the preliminary revolution . . . The extraordinary and immense power of the Bolsheviki lies in the fact that the Kerensky government absolutely ignored the desires of the masses as expressed in the Bolsheviki program of peace, land and workers' control of industry.[4]

The "proletariat, the soldiers and peasants lined up against the bour-geoisie": This was the essence of the Russian Revolution. October was not a coup conducted by a secretive and elitist band. Above all, the revo-lution was about the mobilization of the mass of ordinary Russians—workers, soldiers and peasants—in a struggle to change their world. That is to this day the most important legacy of the Russian Revolution. And this is why such considerable effort is still devoted to distort, slander and misrepresent the events of 1917. This article does not pretend to take up all questions of the revolution—let alone what went wrong—but aims to outline its main themes.[5]

In the autumn of 1932, a Danish Social Democratic student group invited exiled Russian revolutionary Leon Trotsky to speak in Copenhagen on the occasion of the fifteenth anniversary of the Russian Revolution. This speech stands out as one of the most forceful and con-cise accounts of the October Revolution.[6]

Trotsky outlined a series of historical prerequisites necessary for the October Revolution:

1. The rotting away of the old ruling classes—the nobility, the monar-chy, the bureaucracy.

2. The political weakness of the bourgeoisie, which had no roots in the masses of the people.
3. The revolutionary character of the peasant question.
4. The revolutionary character of the problem of the oppressed nations.
5. The significant weight of the proletariat.

To these organic preconditions we must add certain conjunctural conditions of the highest importance.

6. The revolution of 1905 was a great school, or in Lenin's words, the "dress rehearsal" of the revolution of 1917. The soviets, as the irreplaceable organizational form of the proletarian united front in the revolution, were created for the first time in the year 1905.
7. The imperialist war sharpened all the contradictions, tore the backward masses out of their immobility and thereby prepared the grandiose scale of the catastrophe.

But all these conditions, which fully sufficed for the *outbreak of the revolution*, were insufficient to *assure the victory of the revolution*. For this victory one condition more was needed:

8. The Bolshevik Party

This article will try to elucidate these basic features outlined by Trotsky.

The coming of the revolution

Imperial Russia lumbered into the twentieth century a much weakened power than it had been one hundred or even fifty years earlier. Russia had lost considerable ground both militarily and economically relative to its main rivals. The government of Alexander II, in the wake of Russia's defeat in the Crimean War, took steps to implement reforms— to modernize the economy, to modernize the ancient legal system, to "de-feudalize" the army by making service compulsory, to allow a certain degree of local autonomy. In short, it tried to drag Russia out of its medieval past. But the measures adopted were often half-hearted and designed to prolong the status quo rather than change it. Thus, explaining the decision to abolish serfdom in 1861, Alexander II said he decided to end serfdom because "it is better to get rid of serfdom from on high than wait for its abolition from below."[7] Of course this was true, but it overlooked the fact that the key institution that needed overhauling was the autocracy itself. The strength of the autocracy, the servility of the nobility and the relative weakness of the bourgeoisie were key factors in explaining Russia's growing economic gap with the other European powers. And while there was a spurt of industrial growth in the last two decades of the nineteenth century, this was in the main organized and carried out by the tsarist state.

The state was also the main beneficiary of the program of reforms and grew even more powerful in relation to the nobility and bourgeoisie. As Marcel Liebman put it: "The nobility was politically sterile, the bourgeoisie utterly impotent. The entire history of Russia was molded by this negative factor, by the absence of vigorous or even viable social classes and so counterbalancing the weight of the autocracy."[8] The defects of such an antiquated setup were exposed even more clearly given the mediocrity and incompetence of those who were born to run it—the tsars themselves.

Throughout the nineteenth century they were men without vision, courage or imagination. Their hatred of the intelligentsia was but a reflection of their own intellectual incapacity. "Brute force had become a vigor, and the most hidebound conservatism served them all for a political creed and a program."[9]

The reforms that were designed to restore Russia's might would instead contribute to tsarism's downfall. The effect, for example, of the attempt to maintain Russia as a "Great Power" would be profound domestically and internationally. As one historian put it: "[O]ne result of this was the effort to sustain the armed forces and defense industries of a modern great power strained both the Russian economy and domestic political stability. In addition, relative backwardness called into question the empire's ability to survive in a war against the other powers."[10]

To focus only on Russia's economic backwardness in understanding the course of events would be mistaken. The key to understanding Russia, as Leon Trotsky argued so well, is the combination of the backward *and* the advanced, the old *and* the new. In Trotsky's words:

> Russia's development is first of all notable for its backwardness. But historical backwardness does not mean a mere retracing of the course of the advanced countries a hundred or two hundred years later. Rather it gives rise to an utterly different "combined" social formation, in which the most highly developed achievements of capitalist technique and structure are integrated into the social relations of feudal and pre-feudal

barbarism, transforming and dominating them, fashioning a unique relationship of classes.[11]

The consequences of such *uneven* and *combined* development are made clear by looking at Russia's economy. Trotsky points out that while "peasant cultivation as a whole remained, right up to the revolution, at the level of the seventeenth century, Russian industry in its technique and capitalist structure stood at the level of the advanced countries, and in certain respects even outstripped them."[12] This "combined development" in Russia produced a bourgeoisie that was weak and heavily dependent on the tsarist state and foreign capital for investment. It also produced a working class, though small in size, that was highly concentrated in the most modern enterprises. In 1914, 54 percent of workers in Russia were employed in factories of over five hundred, whereas in the United States the figure was 32.5 percent. The Putilov metal works, which employed thirty thousand workers in 1917, was the largest factory in the world at the time. In Petrograd, 60 percent of the workforce was metalworkers.[13]

Trotsky summarized the importance of the character of Russia's development in understanding the October revolution in these words:

> The first and most general explanation is: Russia a backward country, but only a part of the world economy, only an element of the capitalist world system. In this sense Lenin exhausted the riddle of the Russian Revolution with the lapidary formula, "The chain broke at its weakest link."

Trotsky goes on:

> But the young, fresh, determined proletariat of Russia still constituted only a tiny minority of the nation. The reserves of its revolutionary power lay outside of the proletariat itself—in the peasantry, living in half-serfdom, and in the oppressed nationalities.
>
> The subsoil of the revolution was the agrarian question. The old feudal-monarchic system became doubly intolerable under the conditions of the new capitalist exploitation. The peasant communal areas amounted to some 140 dessiatines.[14] But thirty thousand large landowners, whose average holdings were over two thousands dessiatines, owned altogether 70 million dessiatines, that is, as much as some 10 million peasant families or 50 million of the peasant population. *These statistics of land tenure constituted a ready-made program of agrarian revolt.*
>
> In order for the Soviet state to come into existence, therefore, it was necessary for two factors of different historical nature to collaborate: the

peasant war, that is, a movement which is characteristic of the dawn of bourgeois development, and the proletarian insurrection, that is, a movement which announces the decline of the bourgeois movement. Precisely therein consists the combined character of the Russian Revolution.[15]

Russia's revolutionary movement

The combined character of Russia's economic development also affected the development of politics and culture in Russia. Again, Trotsky explains:

> Precisely because of its historical tardiness, Russia proved to be the only European country in which Marxism, as a doctrine, and the Social-Democracy, as a party, enjoyed a powerful development even prior to the bourgeois revolution—and naturally so, because the problem of the relation between the struggle for democracy and the struggle for socialism were subjected to the most profound theoretical examination in Russia.[16]

The works of Karl Marx and Frederick Engels became available in Russia because the censor opined that they were "an abstract speculation" and therefore of little relevance for Russia. Their works would help shape Russia's revolutionary movement, but not quite in the way they had expected. The main current among Russian revolutionaries, the Narodniks (or populists), took Marx's denunciation of capitalism as showing that Russia would be better off if it could bypass capitalism altogether. The populists argued that the peasant *mir* or traditional commune could become the basis of moving straight to a socialist society.

The later generations of populists, perhaps best represented by an organization called Zemlya I Volya (land and freedom), vacillated between two strategies—both of which started with the assumption that the populists would act *on behalf* of the people. They went "to the people" and tried to foment peasant rebellion, and when that failed they took matters into their own hands and launched a campaign of terror against the tsar and his government.

The development of Marxism in Russia was very much *influenced by*, and developed *against*, the ideas of the populist movement. While Lenin accurately described populism as reactionary (in its historic philosophical sense) he also acknowledged the important role it played in the development of a revolutionary movement in Russia.

The break with populism and the turn to the working class came in 1883, when G. V. Plekhanov founded the Emancipation of Labor Group.

Plekhanov had enthusiastically endorsed militant populism which tried to rouse the peasantry. But by the 1880s several factors led him towards Marxism. First, despite considerable heroism on the part of idealistic revolutionaries, the great hopes of Zemlya I Volya failed to ignite a social revolution, or even to produce any revolutionary activity among the peasants.

Second, after the failure of Zemlya I Volya, populism took a turn to individual terror, which Plekhanov rejected. Third, Plekhanov began to doubt the economic viability of the peasant commune as the basis of a new society. And, fourth, a newly emerging industrial working class began to make itself felt, leading Plekhanov to see workers as the key force in Russia's revolution.

Plekhanov developed what became the basic ideas of Russian Social Democracy (synonymous with revolutionary Marxism today). Two propositions of Plekhanov's deserve mention.

Plekhanov argued that because the productive forces were too low, the immediate political objective of the proletariat had to be the victory of the democratic or bourgeois revolution. But Russia's bourgeoisie, a diminutive late-comer, was not going to lead such a struggle or even give the struggle consistent support. Echoing Marx, Plekhanov argued "that whenever the 'red specter' took at all a threatening form, the 'liberals' were ready to seek protection in the embraces of the most unceremonious military dictatorship." This led Plekhanov to the central operational question. "In conclusion," he wrote, "I repeat—and I insist upon this important point: the revolutionary movement in Russia will triumph only as a working-class movement or it will never triumph!"[17]

For ten years after its founding in 1883, the Emancipation of Labor Group remained largely an exile organization. But it nevertheless played a tremendous role in spreading the ideas of Marxism within émigré circles and in Russia itself. By the early 1890s, Marxist study circles, composed primarily of students and intellectuals, existed in many Russian cities and towns. Vladimir Ilych Ulyanov—Lenin—the future leader of the Bolshevik Party, joined such a group when he moved to St. Petersburg in 1893.

Lenin was typical in many respects of the second generation of Russian Marxists. Initially attracted to populism, he was profoundly influenced by Plekhanov's critique *and* by the growing ferment among Russian workers. In this period, Lenin's efforts were directed in the main to fusing Marxism with the working-class movement. Lenin believed that "by directing socialism towards a fusion with the working-class movement, Karl Marx and Frederick Engels did their greatest service," because the previous "separation of the working-class movement and socialism gave rise to weakness and underdevelopment in each: the theories of the socialist, unfused with the workers' struggle, remained nothing more than utopias, good wishes that had no effect on real life; the working-class movement remained petty, fragmented, and did not acquire political significance, was not enlightened by the advanced science of its time."[18]

Therefore, Lenin concluded, "the task of Social-Democracy is to bring definite socialist ideals to the spontaneous working-class movement, to connect this movement with socialist convictions that should attain the level of contemporary science, to connect it with the regular political struggle for democracy as a means of achieving socialism—in a word, to fuse this spontaneous movement into one indestructible whole with the activity of the *revolutionary party*."[19]

Marxism, for Lenin, was therefore, not simply a set of economic laws or doctrines, nor simply a world view, but a guide to action which had definite practical implications.

Marxism makes clear "the real task of a revolutionary socialist party: not to draw up plans for refashioning society, not to preach to the capitalists and their hangers-on about improving the lot of the workers, not to hatch conspiracies, *but to organize the class struggle of the proletariat and to lead this struggle, the ultimate aim of which is the conquest of political power by the proletariat and the organization of a socialist society.*"[20]

Lenin's conclusions were not shared by all Marxists at the time. Indeed, the very success of the Marxist study circles' turn to agitation in the latter 1890s produced a distinctly "anti-political" current, Economism, which glorified the economic struggles of the proletariat. This current, echoing the "revisionism" of the German Socialist leader Eduard Bernstein, who argued "the movement is everything, the final goal nothing," aimed to limit workers to purely economic struggles, leaving the political struggle to the liberals. In these views, the Economists were the political forerunners of the Mensheviks, who formed the moderate wing of Russian socialism after a split in 1903.

Lenin responded to the Economist challenge by arguing against the arbitrary separation of economics and politics. It would be counterproductive for a revolutionary to "adapt himself to the lowest level of understanding" in a manner that would "put the 'demands and interests of the given moment' in the foreground and . . . push back the broad ideas of socialism and the political struggle." Revolutionaries should rather "connect socialism and the political struggle with every local and narrow question."[21]

Lenin's words have tremendous relevance and meaning for socialists today. Revolutionary socialists, he argued, should not simply talk to workers about factory conditions and workplace struggles, but also about the "brutal treatment of the people by the police, the persecution of religious sects, the flogging of peasants, the outrageous censorship, the torture of soldiers, the persecution of the most innocent cultural undertakings, etc." The reasons for making sure that political agitation of this kind is carried out are not based on some abstract "Marxist" principles, but flow directly from what is needed in the struggle. Working-class consciousness "cannot be genuine political consciousness," Lenin further argued, "unless the workers are trained to respond to all cases of tyranny, oppression, violence, and abuse, no matter what class is affected—unless they are trained, moreover, to respond from a Social Democratic point of view and no other."[22]

These ideas would become the cornerstone of the revolutionary wing of the Russian socialist movement—the Bolsheviks.

Three views of the Russian Revolution

It was widely accepted among Russia's Marxist revolutionaries that the coming Russian revolution would be a bourgeois revolution. The founding congress of the Russian Social Democratic Labor Party, stated:

> The further east one goes in Europe, the meaner, more cowardly and politically weak the bourgeoisie becomes, and the greater are the cultural and political tasks that fall to the proletariat. On its own sturdy shoulders the Russian working class must, and will, carry the cause of the achievement of political liberty. This is an essential step, but only an initial step, to the realization of the great historic mission of the proletariat, the creation of a social order in which there will be no place for the exploitation of man by man.[23]

Russia was an economically backward country, with a weak bourgeoisie, a weak industrial base and a small working class. The country was overwhelmingly agricultural with only four to five million industrial workers out of a total population of 160 million.

The Mensheviks argued that because the revolution was a bourgeois one, its leadership belonged to the bourgeoisie. The working class would have to consciously subordinate its demands and interests to those of the bourgeoisie. The Mensheviks drew direct parallels between the Russian bourgeoisie and the bourgeoisie of France at the time of the French Revolution of 1789. It was a vital imperative for the Mensheviks that all be done to safeguard the interests of the bourgeoisie and to make sure that they were not frightened by the prospects of a movement from below.

The role of social democracy was to "exert revolutionary pressure on the will of the liberal and radical bourgeoisie," and "to force the upper strata of society to lead the bourgeois revolution to its logical conclusions."[24]

Lenin and the Bolsheviks did not challenge the idea that the Russian revolution would be bourgeois. "The democratic revolution will not extend beyond the scope of the bourgeois social-economic relationships," wrote Lenin.[25] He maintained this position until mid-1917.

But unlike the Mensheviks, Lenin refused to subordinate the demands of the working class to those of the bourgeoisie or to compromise the independence of the labor movement politically and organizationally. Though Russia's economic level permitted only a bourgeois revolution, the development of a combative working class meant that the bourgeoisie would be incapable of taking the lead:

> The bourgeoisie as a whole is incapable of waging a determined struggle against the autocracy; it fears to lose in this struggle its property which binds it to the existing order; it fears an all-too-revolutionary action of the workers, who will not stop at the democratic revolution but will aspire to the socialist revolution; it fears a complete break with officialdom, with the bureaucracy, whose interests are bound up by a thousand ties with the interests of the propertied classes. For this reason the bourgeois struggle for liberty is notoriously timorous, inconsistent and half-hearted.[26]

Because of this, Lenin argued, the working class would take the lead in the democratic revolution. He went on to argue that since the peasantry had a real interest in ending tsarism and destroying the remnants of feudalism, the "only force capable of gaining 'a decisive victory over Tsarism' is the people, i.e., the proletariat and the peasantry. . . . The revolution's 'decisive victory over Tsarism' means the establishment of the revolutionary democratic dictatorship of the proletariat and the peasantry.

But of course it will be democratic, not a socialist dictatorship ... At best, it may bring about a radical redistribution of landed property in favor of the peasantry, establish consistent and full democracy, including the formation of a republic ... and—last but not least—carry 'the revolution-ary conflagration' into Europe. Such a victory will not yet by any means transform our bourgeois revolution into a socialist revolution.[27]

Leon Trotsky rejected the Mensheviks' reliance on the Russian bour-geoisie as strongly as the Bolsheviks. But this led him to conclusions quite different from those of Lenin.

Following Marx (and largely in agreement with the Menshevik theo-reticians) he argued that the peasantry would not play an independent political role in the revolution.

the peasantry cannot play a leading revolutionary role. ... Because of its dispersion, political backwardness, and especially of its deep inner con-tradictions which cannot be resolved within the framework of a capitalist system, the peasantry can only deal the old order some powerful blows from the rear, by spontaneous risings in the countryside, on the one hand, and by creating discontent within the army on the other.[28]

Because "the town leads in modern society," only an urban class can play the leading role and because the bourgeoisie was not revolutionary, this role fell to the working class:

The conclusion remains that only the proletariat in its class struggle, plac-ing the peasant masses under its revolutionary leadership, can 'carry the revolution to the end.'[29]

But if the working class must lead the revolution, then the working class cannot be expected to stop its struggle after the overthrow of the autocracy. Lenin's "democratic dictatorship" is an impossibility.

The political domination of the proletariat is incompatible with its eco-nomic enslavement. No matter under what political flag the proletariat has come to power, it is obliged to take the path of socialist policy. It would be the greatest utopianism to think that the proletariat, hav-ing been raised to political domination by the internal mechanism of a bourgeois revolution can, even if it so desires, limit its mission to the creation of republican-democratic conditions for the social domination of the bourgeoisie.[30]

But this proposition clearly leads to a difficulty—one that all Russian Marxists understood: Russia was economically and culturally too backward for socialism. How did Trotsky propose to overcome this problem? Given that Russia *in isolation* did not have the economic prerequisites to build socialism, the Russian Revolution would have to be a prelude to revolutions in Europe and elsewhere.

> The Russian revolution will become the first stage of the socialist world revolution.
>
> The present productive forces have long outgrown their national limits. A socialist society is not feasible within national boundaries. Significant as the economic successes of an isolated workers' state may be, the program of socialism in one country is a petty bourgeois utopia. Only a European and then a world federation of socialist republics can be the real arena for a harmonious socialist society.[31]

Trotsky called his analysis the theory of "permanent revolution."

The revolution of 1905

The revolution of 1905 was the first mass rising against the imperial regime. It was, in Lenin's words, the "great dress rehearsal" for 1917. All of the elements of 1917 were there in less developed form. Russia was embroiled in a losing war with Japan, and troop discontent mingled with peasants' desire for land and the mass strikes of workers in the main cities for economic and political rights. Also of critical importance was the emergence of the soviets—or workers' councils—which first made their appearance in St. Petersburg at the height of the revolution.

The revolution began in January 1905 with Bloody Sunday—when the tsar's troops massacred more than eight hundred workers in a mass procession to humbly ask the tsar for reforms. This led to an explosion of mass strikes, mutinies in the army and scattered peasant revolts. It ended in December of that year with a failed uprising in Moscow under the slogan "the eight hour day and a gun," inspired and led by the Bolsheviks. Though it ended in defeat, 1905 was also significant because it cemented the political differences between the Mensheviks, who concluded that the revolution had "gone too far" and had therefore frightened the bourgeoisie into the arms of reaction, and the Bolsheviks, who were confirmed in their view that only the independent mass struggle of workers could carry the revolution to success.

The soviet was a kind of workers' government, made up of elected delegates from Petrograd's factories and workplaces, concentrating all the forces of the revolution. Wrote Trotsky, its president:

> It was an organization which was authoritative and yet had no traditions; which would immediately involve a scattered mass of hundreds of thousands of people while having virtually no organizational machinery; which united the revolutionary currents within the proletariat; which was capable of initiative and spontaneous self-control—and, most of all, which could be brought out from underground within twenty-four hours.[32]

The soviet's premises, wrote Trotsky,

> were always crowded with petitioners and plaintiffs of all kinds—mostly workers, domestic servants, shop assistants, peasants, soldiers and sailors. Some had an absolutely phantasmagorical idea of the Soviet's power and its methods. There was one blind veteran of the Russo-Turkish war, covered with crosses and decorations, who complained of dire poverty and begged the Soviet to "put a little pressure on Number One" [that is, the tsar].

Trotsky recounts another case where an old Cossack sent the soviet a letter asking for some help with a problem. He addressed the letter "simply to The Workers' Government, Petersburg, yet it was promptly delivered by the revolutionary postal service."[33]

The experience of the revolution's high point—the Soviets, the workers' councils—would not be lost. Nor would the violence unleashed by the state. After the suppression of the Soviet by force, many workers drew a critically important lesson: "In the clashing and creaking of twisting metal one heard the gnashing teeth of a proletariat who for the first time fully realized that a more formidable and more ruthless effort was necessary to overthrow and crush the enemy."[34]

The 1905 revolution did not only expose clearly the character of the revolution in Russia, it also showed in practice what the arguments between Bolsheviks and Mensheviks meant in practice. It exposed the different currents in the movement internationally as well. For example, it sparked a heated debate inside the largest social democratic party—the SPD—in Germany. Rosa Luxemburg brilliantly summed up the revolutionary implications of 1905:

> But for international social democracy, the uprising of the Russian proletariat constitutes something profoundly new which we must feel with

every fiber of our being. All of us, whatever pretensions we have to a mastery of dialectics, remain incorrigible metaphysicians, obsessed by the immanence of everything within our everyday experience. . . . It is only in the volcanic explosion of the revolution that we perceive what swift and earth-shattering results the young mole has achieved and just how happily it is undermining the very ground under the feet of European bourgeois society. Gauging the political maturity and revolutionary energy of the working class through electoral statistics and the membership of local branches is like trying to measure Mont Blanc with a ruler![35]

Finally, 1905 had a massive impact around the world as Julius Braunthal, one of the historians of the Internationals, writes:

> It was an unforgettable experience, this first revolutionary uprising of the workers since the Paris Commune of 1871, and, for many contemporaries, the first experience of revolution. To some it seemed that they were living through a turning-point in world history and witnessing the start of a new epoch of European revolutions.[36]

Years of Reaction

The years after 1905 saw repression on an unprecedented scale. As the repression intensified, it was harder and harder to keep any organization going. One historian writes:

> The movement inside Russia had exhausted itself and its remnants were being methodically cut down by Stolypins' [chairman of the council of ministers] draconian policies. To all intents and purposes the Party as an organized structure had ceased to exist. . . . All the major centers of Social Democratic activity were repeatedly hit by mass arrests followed by an inevitable decline in the number of party members. In Moscow, for instance, where the Bolsheviks had had 2,000 members in 1905, their numbers shrank to 500 by the end of 1908 and by mid-1909 there remained only 260 members of the Party.[37]

Many of the problems facing the party were made worse by the fact that the intellectuals took fright and fled the movement—and were never to return. One worker-Bolshevik, Martsionovsky, a carpenter, wrote:

> In a whole series of cities where I took part in illegal work, almost everywhere the party committee consisted exclusively of workers. The intelligentsia was absent, with the exception of those on tour who came for two or three days. In the most difficult years of the reaction, the workers

remained almost without leaders from the intelligentsia. They said that they were tired. . . . We, the underground workers, had to work without the intelligentsia, with the exception of individuals. But on the other hand, after the February Revolution, they showed up, they beat their breasts and shouted "we are revolutionaries," etc., but in fact, none of them had conducted revolutionary work, and we had not seen them in the underground.[38]

The period between 1911 and the outbreak of World War I saw a revival in militancy and a corresponding growth in the Bolshevik Party. In April 1912, the police fired on a demonstration of striking miners in Lena, Siberia—killing 170 and provoking huge sympathy strikes in Moscow and Petersburg. The revival of the workers' movement is reflected most clearly in the strike statistics for the years leading up to World War I. One study gives the following figures:

Strikes in Russia 1910–1914

Number of Strikes				*Working Days Lost (in thousands)*
	Total	*Economic*	*Political*	
1910	222	214	8	256
1911	466	442	24	791
1912	2,032	732	1,300	2,376
1913	2,404	1,370	1,034	3,863
1914	3,534	969	2,565	5,755[39]

World War 1 and the collapse of tsarism

For many years, the Second International had proclaimed its opposition to militarism and war. The 1907 Resolution of the International Socialist Congress at Stuttgart reads:

If a war threatens to break out it is the duty of the working class and its parliamentary representatives in the countries involved, supported by the consolidating activity of the International [Socialist] Bureau, to exert every effort to prevent the outbreak of war by means they consider most effective, which naturally vary according to the accentuation of the class struggle and of the general political situation.

Should war break out nonetheless, it is their duty to intervene in favor of its speedy termination and to do all in their power to utilize the economic and political crisis caused by the war to rouse the peoples and thereby to hasten the abolition of capitalist class rule.[40]

These resolutions proved hollow. World War I saw the main parties of the Second International abandon the slogans of peacetime and throw their support behind their ruling classes' own war effort. In every belligerent country, the socialist movement split between "social patriots" and "internationalists." The antiwar camp was, in turn, sharply divided between advocates of "peace" and those, like Lenin, who called for revolutionaries to turn the world war into a civil war against their own ruling classes.

For Lenin, the betrayal of principles and the about-face of the German SPD was quite unexpected. When he first heard of the reports that German socialists in the Reichstag had voted for war credits, he did not at first believe them. And the antiwar forces were small. Rosa Luxemburg sent out an antiwar circular to twenty of the most left-wing members of SPD Reichstag group and received only two responses. In 1915, the antiwar socialists met at Zimmerwald in Switzerland and reaffirmed the principles of international socialism. Trotsky wrote of the meeting:

> The delegates, filling four stage-coaches, set off for the mountains. The passers-by looked on curiously at the strange procession. The delegates themselves joked about the fact that half a century after the founding of the First International, it was still possible to seat all the internationalists in four coaches.[41]

But this nucleus also formed the basis of a new, revolutionary international—the Third International. The coming revolutionary storm was to swell the ranks of the revolutionaries into the hundreds of thousands across Russia and Europe.

The war exacerbated the crisis of tsarism in several respects. The scale of the carnage and the human toll it exacted was massive. Trotsky writes in his *History of the Russian Revolution*: "The Russian army lost in the whole war more men than any army which ever participated in a national war—approximately two and a half million killed, or 40 percent of all the losses of the Entente."[42]

The war and its cost domestically began to split the ruling order in Russia. Some, with the tsar at their head, believed the war would cement Russian society through a patriotic outpouring and would stave off social revolution. To make matters worse, the tsar decided to take personal command of the army and war effort in the late summer of 1915. Even members of the tsar's cabinet could no longer ignore the decay and stench. The acting minister of agriculture, A. V. Krivoshein:

> Historians will not believe it, that Russia conducted the war blindly and hence came to the edge of ruin—that millions of men were unconsciously sacrificed for the arrogance of some and the criminality of others. What is going on at headquarters is a universal outrage and horror.[43]

As the war dragged on, it became more and more unpopular—both at home and at the front. In the towns, food shortages became frequent. Inflation and fuel shortages became permanent features of the lives of workers in the cities. Dissent began to grow in the factories and in the army. The Bolshevik leader Shlyapnikov records in his memoirs:

> By the end of 1916 the idea of "war to the end," to the "final victory," was largely undermined. Anti-war feelings were rampant. . . . Despair and hatred gripped the laboring masses. . . . The government . . . stepped up their repressive methods of fighting isolated manifestations of protest. Intensive agitation was conducted against us in the press and through the various organizations working for the "organization of defense." Every resource was set in motion: accusations of provocation, or German intrigues and bribes. But slander could not halt the workers' movement either: just like the bourgeoisie's other ploys it proved incapable of rousing the proletariat to . . . [fight].[44]

A sign of the decline and decay of the autocracy was the growing influence of a drunk mystic, Gregori Rasputin. The tsarina called on Nicholas to act as strongman, but it was too late—even if he'd focused his attention long enough to act decisively. Instead, despondency accompanied decline.

Even the tsar's police could see that a revolution was imminent. At the end of 1916, the police department compared the situation in the main cities to ten years earlier and concluded that "now the mood of opposition has reached such extraordinary proportions as it did by a long way among the broad masses in that troubled time."[45] Trotsky's remark about the 1905 revolution, "Every Paris concierge knew . . . in advance that there was going to a be revolution in Petersburg on Sunday, January 9,"[46] applied equally to 1917. Revolution was in the air, not only because those at the bottom of society wanted a change, but so too did those at the top. In Lenin's words,

> For a revolution to take place, it is not usually sufficient for the 'lower classes not to want' to live in the old way; it is also necessary that the 'upper classes should be unable' to live in the old way.[47]

The February Revolution

The prelude to the February revolution consisted of a series of strikes and demonstrations in Petrograd commemorating Bloody Sunday. The strike movement spread and deepened after workers at the giant Putilov Works were locked out for demanding a wage increase. Even the most militant section of the Bolshevik Party, the Vyborg district, urged that the strikes end for fear that conditions weren't yet ripe for mass, militant action. Then on February 23—International Women's Day—women textile workers poured into the streets of Petrograd demanding bread. As Trotsky explained:

> The 23rd of February was International Women's Day. The social-democratic circles had intended . . . meetings, speeches, leaflets. It had not occurred to anyone that it might become the first day of the revolution. Not a single organization called for strikes that day.[48]

The women textile workers of Petrograd came out on strike and dragged behind them the Bolshevik-led metalworkers of the Vyborg district. As one of the leaders of the Bolshevik Vyborg District Committee, Kayurov, put it, "with reluctance, the Bolsheviks agreed to this."[49] Indeed, Kayurov later remarked that he had tried to talk the women workers out of taking any action at all.[50]

Trotsky remarks, "Thus the fact is that the February revolution was begun from below, overcoming the resistance of its own revolutionary organizations, the initiative being taken of their own accord by the most oppressed and downtrodden part of the proletariat—the women textile workers, among them no doubt many soldiers' wives."[51]

By the end of the day, 90,000 workers were on strike—without the shootings the Bolsheviks had feared. The next day, the 24th, about half of Petrograd's workers were on strike and large numbers of them were demonstrating in the streets. The slogan "Bread!" writes Trotsky, "is crowded out or obscured by louder slogans: 'Down with the autocracy,' 'Down with the war!'" Fearful that the infantry would not obey orders to shoot on unarmed workers, the government brought out its most reliable troops, the Cossack cavalry. The Cossacks did not mutiny, but neither did they act as they were expected to:

> The Cossacks constantly, though without ferocity, kept charging the crowd. . . . The mass of the demonstrators would part to let them through, and close up again. There was no fear in the crowd. "The Cossacks promise not to shoot," passed from mouth to mouth.[52]

The disintegration of the tsar's armed forces was evident to the demonstrators. In the streets of the Nevsky Prospekt in Petrograd a Bolshevik worker and demonstrator saw the front ranks of the crowd, pressed forward by those behind, come closer and closer to a cordon of soldiers:

> The tips of the bayonets were touching the breasts of the first row of demonstrators. Behind could be heard the singing of revolutionary songs, in front there was confusion. Women, with tears in their eyes, were crying out to the soldiers, "Comrades, take away your bayonets, join us!" The soldiers were moved. They threw swift glances at their own comrades. The next moment one bayonet is slowly raised, is slowly lifted above the shoulders of the approaching demonstrators. There is thunderous applause. The triumphant crowd greeted their brothers clothed in the gray cloaks of the soldiery. The soldiers mixed freely with the demonstrators.[53]

Another three days of this and it was all over for the tsar. On the night of the 26th the reserve battalions of the Volynsky Regiment mutinied. The following morning they killed their commanding officer and joined the workers' demonstrations. General Khabalov, commander of the Petrograd military garrison, conceded on the evening of the 27th, saying, ". . . I cannot fulfill the command to re-establish order in the capital. Most of the units one by one have betrayed their duty, refusing to fight the rioters."[54] The speed of the army's mutiny was striking. On February 26 there were six hundred mutineers; three days later the whole Petrograd garrison of 170,000 had rebelled.

On February 26, Michael V. Rodzyanko, president of the lame Duma, wired the tsar:

> Anarchy in the capital, government paralyzed . . . shooting in the streets . . . supplies of food and fuel completely disrupted . . . universal dissatisfaction growing . . . there must be no delay in forming a new government enjoying the confidence of the country. Any hesitation would

mean death. I pray to God that in this hour no responsibility falls on the monarch.[55]

The tsar's reply was to delay the opening of the Duma. Its members were at a loss. "I do not want to revolt," exclaimed Rodzyanko.

I am no rebel. I have made no revolution and do not intend to make one. . . . I am no revolutionary. I will not rise up against the supreme power. I do not want to. But there is no government any longer. Everything falls to me. . . . All the phones are ringing. Everybody asks me what to do. What shall I say? Shall I step aside? Wash my hands in innocence? Leave Russia without a government? After all, it is Russia! Have we not a duty to our country? What shall I do? Tell me, what?[56]

In the end, Rodzyanko sent another telegram pleading with the tsar to intervene. "Situation worsening. Immediate steps are necessary, for tomorrow it will be too late. The last hour has come in which the fate of the country and the dynasty is being decided." Forever vigilant and astute, the tsar was unmoved. "That fat Rodzyanko has again sent me some nonsense to which I will not even reply," he commented to Count Fredericks, minister of the court.[57]

The tsar's imbecility achieved a truly remarkable feat: it forced a majority of the Duma's members to go against his wishes. Not wanting to offend, they refused to disperse, but met only in an unofficial capacity. Rodzyanko, who contemplated the possibility of the tsar's abdication with "unspeakable sadness," had just advised tsarist authorities to use their firehoses to disperse demonstrators. But the situation needed resolution. At midnight on February 27, the Duma's leaders proclaimed the formation of a provisional government. Their intent was clear. As the leader of the bourgeois Cadet Party, Miliukov, put it: "to direct into a peaceful channel the transfer of power which it had preferred to receive, not from below, but from above." The Duma had no choice but "to take power into its own hands and try to curb the growing anarchy," wrote Rodzyanko.[58] As the Duma leaders proclaimed a new government, the last of the Romanovs recorded the proud achievements of his last night in power: "read a great deal about Julius Caesar" and slept "long and deeply."[59] Three centuries of Romanovs finally came to an ignominious end—the tsar abdicated on March 2.

The February revolution brought a bourgeois government headed by Prince Lvov to office—but it also created another center of power: the Soviet of Workers' and Soldiers' Deputies. Indeed, in the first days after the fall of the tsar, effective power was in the hands of the Soviets. The old state had collapsed and the bourgeoisie was reluctant to take power. But so too was the leadership of the Soviets—then in the hands of the Mensheviks and the peasant party, the Social Revolutionaries (SRs). In their view, the aim of the revolution was the achievement of a bourgeois democratic republic. They were ready and eager to support the new government to see that the tasks of the "bourgeois revolution" were carried out. As the Menshevik Potresov expressed it: "at the moment of the bourgeois revolution, the [class] best prepared, socially and psychologically, to solve national problem is [the] bourgeoisie."[60]

The new government was above all concerned with a return to order: restoring the authority of the officers in the army and of management over workers in industrial enterprises over the workers. Before declaring a provisional government they aptly called themselves "The Committee for the Re-establishment of Order and Relations with Public Institutions and Personages." Their sole preoccupation was stabilizing Russian society—and of course to carrying on the war. Until that time, the other issues raised by the revolution—land reform, the demands of the non-Russian nationalities, the election of a Constituent Assembly, and so on, could all wait. One historian summarizes the approach of the new Provisional Government to the crisis it inherited:

> How did the government deal with the problems it had inherited? It prolonged the war and trod in the Tsar's footsteps. To continue Tsarist foreign policy and combine it with an adventurous military offensive would, it was hoped, divert attention from the problems of the home front. In Chernov's words—"The propertied classes regarded a military victory and its concomitant chauvinism as the only way to avoid aggravation of the social revolution."[61]

Right up to its overthrow in October, the Provisional Government would doggedly stick to prosecuting the war—effectively laying the basis for its undoing. "If the revolution did not finish the war," wrote the Menshevik Sukhanov, "then the war would strangle the revolution."[62]

But the provisional government also had a big problem. It didn't have the power to rule on its own. As the minister of war and the navy, Guchkov, wrote to the commander in chief, General Alekseev, on March 9:

> The Provisional Government has no real authority at its disposal and its decrees are carried out only to the extent this is permitted by the

Soviet of Workers' and Soldiers' Deputies which has in its hands the most important elements of real power, such as the army, the railways, the post and telegraph. . . . In particular, it is now possible to give only these orders which do not radically conflict with the orders of the above-named Soviet.[63]

Reorienting the Bolshevik Party

Bolshevik Party leaders in Russia during the February revolution largely accommodated to the Menshevik-SR political line. They clung to the notion that the Russian Revolution had to limit itself to bourgeois aims. They tried to take a verbally critical stance, but effectively served as the left face of the soviet majority, which itself covered for the Provisional Government. The new editors of *Pravda*, Kamenev and Stalin, who returned from exile in Siberia, "Pronounced that the Bolsheviks would decisively support the Provisional Government 'insofar as it struggles against reaction or counter-revolution' forgetting that the only important agent of counter-revolution at the time was this same Provisional Government," writes Tony Cliff caustically.[64] Although there was considerable opposition within the party to the political line adopted towards the Provisional Government, it would take Lenin's return from exile, on April 3, 1917, to decisively shift the party—indeed, the whole course of the revolution.

At a meeting in March of the Provisional Government, when ministers were discussing Bolshevik agitation, Kerensky blurted out: "Just wait, Lenin himself is coming. Then the real thing will start."[65] The "real thing" did indeed start—but in a way no one anticipated.

Lenin arrived at the Finland railway station—which was located in the Bolshevik stronghold of the Vyborg district. Like Plekhanov, who had returned a few days earlier, Lenin was welcomed by a group of dignitaries including Chkheidze, the Menshevik chair of the Petrograd Soviet. The description of the official meeting deserves to be quoted in full, despite its length:

> Behind Shlyapnikov, at the head of a small cluster of people behind whom the door slammed again at once, Lenin came, or rather ran, into the room. He wore a round cap, his face looked frozen, and there was a magnificent bouquet in his hands. Running to the middle of the room, he stopped in front of Chkheidze as though colliding with a completely unexpected obstacle. And Chkheidze, still glum, pronounced the following "speech of

welcome" with not only the spirit and wording but also the tone of a sermon. "Comrade Lenin, in the name of the Petersburg Soviet and of the whole revolution we welcome you to Russia. . . . But—we think that the principal task of the revolutionary democracy is now the defense of the revolution from any encroachments either from within or from without. We consider that what this goal requires is not disunity, but the closing of the democratic ranks. We hope you will pursue these goals together with us."

Chkheidze stopped speaking. I was dumbfounded with surprise: really, what attitude could be taken to this "welcome" and to that delicious "But—"

But Lenin knew exactly how to behave. He stood there as though nothing taking place had the slightest connection with him—looking about him, examining the persons round him and even the ceiling of the imperial waiting-room, adjusting his bouquet (rather out of tune with his whole appearance), and then, turning away from the Ex. Com. delegation altogether, he made this reply:

"Dear comrades, soldiers, sailors, and workers! I am happy to greet in your persons the victorious Russian revolution, and greet you as the vanguard off the worldwide proletarian army. . . . The piratical imperialist war is the beginning of civil war throughout Europe. . . . The hour is not far distant when at the call of our [German] comrade, Karl Liebknecht, the people will turn their arms against their own capitalist exploiters. . . . The worldwide socialist revolution has already dawned. . . . Germany is seething. . . . Any day now the whole of European capitalism may crash. The Russian revolution accomplished by you has prepared the way and opened a new epoch. Long live the worldwide socialist revolution!"

Appealing from Chkheidze to the workers and soldiers, from the provisional government to Liebknecht, from the defense of the fatherland to international revolution—this is how Lenin indicated the tasks of the proletariat.[66]

Sukhanov summed up Lenin's speech to a Bolshevik Party meeting that day:

I shall never forget that thunder-like speech, which startled and amazed not only me, a heretic who had accidentally dropped in, but all the true believers. I am certain that no one had expected anything of the sort.[67]

The response to Lenin's speech was that of stunned silence. He was denounced from all sides. "A man who talks that kind of stupidity is not dangerous," exclaimed Stakevich, a moderate socialist. Bogdanov, a

Menshevik: "That is raving, the ravings of a lunatic! It is indecent to applaud this claptrap!" A member of the Bolsheviks, Zalezhki, noted: "On that day (April 4) Comrade Lenin could not find open sympathizers even in our own ranks." Lenin's speech, she remembers, "produced on everyone a stupefying impression. No one expected this. On the contrary, they expected Vladimir Ilych to arrive and call to order the Russian Bureau of the Central Committee and especially Comrade Molotov, who occupied a particularly irreconcilable position with respect to the Provisional Government.[68]

On April 9, *Pravda*, the Bolshevik party newspaper, ran an editorial attacking Lenin written by Central Committee member, L. B. Kamenev:

> As for the general *schema* of Lenin, its seems to us unacceptable in that it starts from the assumption that the bourgeois-democratic revolution is ended and counts upon an immediate transformation of this revolution into a socialist revolution.[69]

But Lenin refused to be cowed. He launched an attack of his own. As he had done in 1905, he attacked those "old Bolsheviks" who continued to apply policies and methods which were appropriate for one period, but now acted as a hindrance to the aims of the revolution. For example, he attacked Kamenev's "old Bolshevik" formula that "the bourgeois revolution is not completed" as "obsolete." "It is no good at all. It is dead. And it is no use trying to revive it." He criticized the old Bolsheviks for refusing to abandon the formula of the "revolutionary-democratic dictatorship of the proletariat and the peasantry"—which was his slogan at the start of the 1905 revolution. Those who wanted to hang on to that idea, said Lenin, "should be consigned to the archive of 'Bolshevik'" pre-revolutionary antiques (it may be called the archive of 'Old Bolsheviks').[70]

Lenin answered his critics by hammering home the central point: the workers can only rely on themselves.

> Ours is a bourgeois revolution, *therefore*, the workers must support the bourgeoisie, say the Potresovs, Gvozdyovs and Chkheidzes, as Plekhanov said yesterday.
>
> Ours is a bourgeois revolution, we Marxists say, *therefore* the workers must open the eyes of the people to the deception practiced by the bourgeois politicians and teach them to put no faith in words, to depend entirely on their own strength, their own organization, their own unity, and their own weapons.[71]

In effect, Lenin was adopting Trotsky's "permanent revolution" position. The first stage of the revolution had created a situation of "dual power," in which the working class and rebellious soldiers were not yet conscious of the need to sweep away the bourgeois Provisional Government. The task now was to win over a majority of the proletariat to the side of Bolshevism.

> No support for the Provisional Government.... Exposure (of) the impermissible, illusion-breeding "demand" that this government, a government of capitalists, should cease to be an imperialist government.... The masses must be made to see that the Soviets of Workers' Deputies are the only possible form of revolutionary government, and that therefore our task is, as long as this government yields to the influence of the bourgeoisie, to present a patient, systematic and persistent explanation of the errors of their tactics, an explanation especially adapted to the needs of the masses. As long as we are in a minority we carry on the work of criticizing and exposing errors and at the same time we preach the necessity of transferring the entire state power to the Soviets of Workers' Deputies so that the people may overcome their mistakes by experience. Not a parliamentary republic . . . but a republic of Soviets of Workers', Agricultural Laborers and Peasants' Deputies throughout the country, from top to bottom.[72]

Lenin's isolation among the leaders of the Bolsheviks can be gauged by the outcome of a debate and vote on Lenin's views at a Petrograd Committee meeting on April 8. Those opposing Lenin handily won the vote thirteen to two, with one abstention. Similar results were recorded in Moscow and other local Bolshevik committees.[73]

But several factors worked in Lenin's favor. First, many of the rank-and-file members of the party were already unhappy with the line of accommodation to the Provisional Government being pushed by Kamenev, Stalin and the former Duma deputy M. K. Muranov. Indeed some members in Petrograd had called for their expulsion from the party.

Moreover, even if the Bolsheviks' Petrograd leadership tailed behind the Mensheviks and SRs, the Bolshevik members did not have the same instincts as those of the Mensheviks. As Trotsky notes, the whole history and training of the Bolsheviks led them in the direction of identifying with the masses rather than the new bourgeois government. Trotsky writes:

> The worker-Bolsheviks immediately after the revolution took the initiative in the struggle for the eight-hour day; the Mensheviks declared this

demand untimely. The Bolsheviks took the lead in arresting the Tsarist officials; the Mensheviks opposed "excesses." The Bolsheviks energetically undertook the creation of a workers' militia; the Mensheviks delayed the arming of the workers, not wishing to quarrel with the bourgeoisie. Although not yet overstepping the bounds of bourgeois democracy, the Bolsheviks acted, or strove to act—however confused by their leadership—like uncompromising revolutionists. The Mensheviks sacrificed their democratic program at every step in the interests of a coalition with the liberals.[74]

Second, the very course of the revolution, and in particular the government's continued escalation to the war effort, was a confirmation of the validity of Lenin's views. Third, the numbers of workers, soldiers and peasants drawn into the revolution continued to grow—as did their hostility to the government and their gravitation to the Bolsheviks; fourth, the Bolshevik Party itself entered a period of explosive growth. In the two months since February, party membership swelled from 24,000 to 80,000. Finally, Lenin carried enormous political weight among the cadres of the Bolshevik Party. Indeed, Trotsky is undoubtedly right in saying that only Lenin could have reoriented the party so quickly and with so little damage. By mid-April, Lenin's attempts to win over the party reached an important turning point: He succeeded in winning a majority at a conference of Bolsheviks held in Petrograd on April 14. By the end of April, Lenin had decidedly won the party over to his views.

No sooner had Lenin won the party over did the opposite danger come to the fore. The same militants who supported Lenin's "no support for the Provisional Government" slogan tended to be involved in head-on clashes with the government. The slogan of "no support" was soon transformed into one of "Down with the Provisional Government." Lenin now swung from the party's left to its right, calling such slogans "premature" and "adventurist." Petrograd's workers were well ahead of the rest of the country, and the danger existed of a premature confrontation with the government which would leave the most militant sections of the movement isolated. The Bolshevik strategy was to rely on peaceful agitation and propaganda to win over a majority in the Soviets. This was the strategy that the Bolsheviks intended to follow, but the actual course of the struggle forced them to adopt a different course.

On May 1, Guchkov, minister of war and the navy, resigned his post from the Provisional Government. He announced that he was no longer able to fulfill his duties because of the continued disintegration and open rebellion in the army: "conditions which I am powerless to alter and which threaten the defense and, freedom and even the existence of Russia with fatal consequences."[75] One graphic symptom of the collapse of the Russian army was the ever-rising number of deserters. The total number of registered deserters (as opposed to a much larger but unknown total number of deserters) from the outbreak of war to February 1917 was 195,130, or 3,423 per fortnight. From the beginning of the revolution to May 15, the number rose to 85,921, or 17,185 per fortnight.[76]

The collapse of the army was one reflection of the growing rebellion among peasants throughout the country. Writes Lionel Kochan: "The storm in the countryside burst in April. Statistics, necessarily incomplete, show an unmistakable and sudden upsurge. In March the number of districts affected by peasant disorders had been 34; in April it was 174; in May 236; in June 280; and in July 325."[77]

The government's response to this crisis was to try to expand its base of support—especially among the Mensheviks and the SRs who still held a majority in the Soviets. In late April, these parties entered the Provisional Government. The right-wing SR Alexander Kerensky became minister of war. From May onwards, the revolutions advance required fighting not only the bourgeoisie, but the leaders of the Mensheviks and SRs. From May to the October seizure of power, there is a visible and steady decline in the levels of support to both Mensheviks and SRs and a sharp swing to the left.

The swing left is best illustrated by the events of the "July Days." Lenin and the Bolshevik leadership had attempted to temper the most militant sections of the party. But this proved no easy task. Already in April, there had been clashes between pro- and anti-government forces, as demonstrations of some 30,000 workers and sailors were organized by the Bolsheviks. On June 9, the Bolsheviks found themselves having to call off a peaceful demonstration in Petrograd where their supporters were going to demand the government resign. The majority in the Soviets, citing the fear of anarchy, had banned the demonstration. The party protested, but submitted. This only infuriated thousands of workers—mainly against the Provisional Government, but many also questioned the party's decision to avoid confrontation. An alternative, official Soviet demonstration held some days later paraded overwhelmingly pro-Bolshevik slogans.

The unavoidable confrontation came in July. Nearly a million demonstrators took to the streets of Petrograd on July 4, demanding an end to the war and the overthrow of the Provisional Government. The Bolsheviks, having failed to restrain the demonstrators, decided to join them. In the confrontations that followed, there were hundreds of casualties. There is little doubt that had the Bolshevik Party called for the overthrow of the government, it could have achieved that aim. But Lenin and others were clear that the rest of Russia wasn't yet ready to overthrow the Provisional Government. Aware of the Bolsheviks' growing strength—and now terrified—the Provisional Government banned the Bolshevik Party. Warrants were issued for the arrest of key leaders of the Bolsheviks, including Lenin and Trotsky. The Bolshevik press was banned and the printing presses smashed to bits. Sukhanov writes in his memoirs that the Bolshevik Party was finished.

But instead, it was the Provisional Government whose days were numbered. With every passing day, it grew more unpopular, its position more tenuous. Bolshevik Party membership increased dramatically—transforming the party completely. In a report to the Sixth Party Congress, held in August, Sverdlov reported that party membership stood at 240,000. The report showed that in Petrograd there were now 41,000 members, as against 15,000 in April. In Moscow 50,900 as against 13,000. By October, the party numbered 350,000.[78]

The growth of the party is all the more remarkable given that the party was virtually driven underground after July. Alongside the repression and intimidation came a well-orchestrated propaganda campaign to discredit and smear the Bolsheviks. Lenin, in particular, was "exposed" as an agent of the Kaiser and anything else they could invent—a slander campaign which is still alive in many history books today! The repression was not strong enough to crush the Bolsheviks. They continued to win members and wider layers of support. The government campaign against the Left had one unintended effect—to virtually finish any base the Mensheviks had among workers. As a historian of the Mensheviks writes:

> A few statistics tell the tale. In June the Mensheviks elected 248 delegates to the first Congress of the Soviets, whereas the Bolsheviks managed to elect only 105. But at the second Congress of the Soviets, which met in October, there were only 70 to 80 Menshevik delegates as against 300 Bolsheviks. During the early stages of the revolution the largest Menshevik organization in Petrograd consisted of 10,000 members; but

by October it had virtually ceased to exist. "Membership dues," so wrote a Menshevik at the time, "were not being paid, the circulation of the *Workers' Gazette* declined catastrophically, the last all-city conference did not take place for lack of a quorum. . . . The withdrawal from the party of groups and individuals is an everyday occurrence."[79]

The government's hard line also helped push large sections of the SRs towards the Bolsheviks. But if the Mensheviks and the SRs no longer had a mass base, they were of no use to the reactionaries that made up the officer caste in the army, to the bourgeoisie or to the middle classes. The call for a military coup from the right began to be raised openly. In mid-August, the Provisional Government tried to muster public support by organizing a State Conference. To protest the conference, the Bolsheviks called a general strike in Moscow that shut much of the city down—yet another sign of the Bolshevik's resurgence from the July repression. During the proceedings General Kornilov, commander in chief, talked about the need to restore order in the army and at "the rear."

> The army is conducting a ruthless struggle against anarchy, and anarchy will be crushed. . . . By a whole series of legislative measures passed after the revolution by people whose understanding and spirit were alien to the army, this army was converted into the most reckless mob, which values nothing but its own life . . . there can be no army without discipline. . . . The prestige of the officers must be enhanced. . . . There is no army without a rear. . . . The measures that are adopted at the front must also be adopted in the rear.[80]

General Kornilov launched a coup attempt in late August. On August 26, he sent a representative to demand the surrender of the Provisional Government. He had the backing of all the top generals, big business and the British and French governments. But Kornilov's coup failed largely because of the organized resistance led by the Bolsheviks.

Lenin's response to the Kornilov revolt was clear and immediate: "The Kornilov revolt is a most unexpected and downright unbelievably sharp turn in events. Like every sharp turn, it calls for a revision and change of tactics."[81] The Bolshevik Party must lead the resistance to Kornilov, Lenin argued, because a successful coup from the right would be a tremendous setback to the revolution. Thus, Bolsheviks and their supporters were organized to fight Kornilov. This did not mean, however, extending support to the government. "*Even now* we must not support

Kerensky's government. This is unprincipled. . . . We shall fight, we are fighting against Kornilov, *just* as Kerensky's *troops* do, but we do not support Kerensky. On the contrary, we expose his weakness.[82]

"We are changing the *form* of our struggle against Kerensky. Without in the least relaxing our hostility towards him, without taking back a single word said against him, without renouncing the task of overthrowing him."[83]

After four days, the coup collapsed. "The insurrection," Trotsky noted, "had rolled back, crumbled to pieces, been sucked up by the earth."[84] The forces of reaction were completely demoralized, and Kornilov's defeat only accelerated the decomposition of the Provisional Government.

The masses on the stage of history

The greatest historian of the revolution, and one of its most important participants, Leon Trotsky, described the significance of revolution:

> The most indubitable feature of a revolution is the direct interference of the masses in historic events. In ordinary times the state, be it monarchical or democratic, elevates itself above the nation, and history is made by specialists in that line of business—kings, ministers, bureaucrats, parliamentarians, journalists. But at those crucial moments when the old order becomes no longer endurable to the masses, they break over the barriers excluding them from the political arena, sweep aside their traditional representatives, and create by their own interference the initial groundwork for a new regime. Whether this is good or bad we leave to the judgment of moralists. We ourselves will take the facts as they are given by the objective course of development. The history of a revolution is for us first of all a history of the forcible entrance of the masses into the realm of rulership over their own destiny.[85]

Passivity gave way to self-activity. As historian Marc Ferro put it, "The citizens of the new Russia, having overthrown Tsardom, were in a state of permanent mobilization." "All Russia," wrote Sukhanov, "was constantly demonstrating in those days."[86]

> The revolution awakened a sense of power in ordinary people.
> From the very depths of Russia came a great cry of hope in which were mingled the voices of the poor and downtrodden, expressing their sufferings, hopes and dreams. Dream-like, they experienced unique events: in Moscow, workmen would compel their employer to learn the bases of

the workers' rights in the future; in Odessa, students would dictate a new way of teaching universal history to their professor; in Petrograd, actors would take over from the theater manager and select the next play; in the army, soldiers would summon the chaplain to attend their meetings so that he could "get some real meaning in his life." Even "children under the age of fourteen" demanded the right to learn boxing "to make the older children have some respect."[87]

No longer were discussions of the main issues facing ordinary workers limited to the privileged and powerful. All questions of politics and economics, of war and peace, of how to organize society, were now the property of the masses. Krupskaya, Lenin's partner, describes the mood:

> The streets in those days presented a curious spectacle: everywhere people stood about in knots, arguing heatedly and discussing the latest events. . . . These street meetings were so interesting, that it once took me three hours to walk from Shirokaya Street to the Krzesinska Mansion. The house in which we lived overlooked a courtyard, and even here, if you opened the window at night, you could hear a heated dispute. A soldier would be sitting there, and he always had an audience—usually some of the cooks, or housemaids from next door, or some young people. An hour after midnight you could catch snatches of talk—"Bolsheviks, Mensheviks. . . . " At three in the morning "Miliukov, Bolsheviks. . . . " At five—still the same street-corner-meeting talk, politics, etc. Petrograd's white nights are always associated in my mind with those all-night political disputes.[88]

John Reed described how the thirst for knowledge and culture was insatiable:

> All Russia was learning to read, and *reading*—politics, economics, history—because the people wanted to *know*. . . . The thirst for education, so long thwarted, burst with the Revolution into a frenzy of expression. From Smolny Institute [headquarters of the Soviet] alone, the first six months, went out every day tons, car-loads, train-loads of literature, saturating the land. Russia absorbed reading matter like hot sand drinks water, insatiable. And it was not fables, falsified history, diluted religion, and the cheap fiction that corrupts—but social and economic theories, philosophy, the works of Tolstoy, Gogol, and Gorky. . . .
> Then the talk . . . Lectures, debates, speeches—in theaters, circuses, school-houses, clubs, Soviet meeting-rooms, union headquarters, barracks. . . . Meetings in the trenches at the Front, in village squares, factories. . . . What a marvelous sight to see Putilovsky Zavod (the Putilov

factory) pour out its forty thousand to listen to Social Democrats, Socialist Revolutionaries, Anarchists, anybody, whatever they had to say, as long as they would talk! For months in Petrograd, and all over Russia, every street-corner was a public tribune. In railway trains, street-cars, always the spurting up of impromptu debate, everywhere. . . .

. . . We came down to the front of the Twelfth Army, back of Riga, where gaunt and bootless men sickened in the mud of desperate trenches; and when they saw us they started up, with their pinched faces and the flesh showing blue through their torn clothing, demanding eagerly, "Did you bring anything to *read*?"[89]

The road to October

On September 1, the Bolsheviks won a majority in the Petrograd Soviet. On September 5, the Moscow Soviet followed suit. On September 9, Trotsky was elected president of the Petrograd Soviet. A clear majority of the working class was behind the Bolsheviks. Lenin launched an offensive within the party to prepare for an armed uprising and seizure of power. He met stiff resistance from the Bolshevik Central Committee. For almost a month, Lenin insistently argued for the party to prepare for an insurrection. Bukharin describes the response of the Central Committee to one of Lenin's letters.

> The letter [of Lenin] was written with extraordinary force and threatened us with all sorts of punishments. We all gasped. Nobody had yet posed the question so abruptly. . . . At first all were bewildered. Afterwards, having talked it over, we made a decision. Perhaps that was the sole case in the history of our party when the Central Committee unanimously decided to burn a letter from Lenin.[90]

Finally, on October 10, after bitter debate, the Central Committee of the Bolshevik Party voted in favor of a rising.

Like every other ruling class, the Russian bourgeoisie and aristocracy thought that nothing and no one could do without it. The conservative daily *Novoe Vromia*, wrote on the morning after the insurrection (October 26, 1917):

> Let us suppose for a moment that the Bolsheviks do gain the upper hand. Who will govern us then: the cooks perhaps, those connoisseurs of cutlets and beefsteaks? Or maybe the firemen? The stable boys, the chauffeurs? Or perhaps the nursemaids will rush off to a meeting of the Council of

State between the diaper washing sessions? Who then? Where are the statesmen? Perhaps the mechanics will run the theaters, the plumbers foreign affairs, the carpenters, the post office. Who will it be? History alone will give a definitive answer to this mad ambition of the Bolsheviks.[91]

The principal responsibility for organizing the insurrection fell to Trotsky, who, as president of the soviet and head of the Military-Revolutionary Committee (formed originally during the Kornilov revolt), organized the insurrection. The actual seizure of power involved relatively small numbers of people and had the trappings of a military operation. As Sukhanov wrote, the broad masses

> had nothing to do on the streets. They did not have an enemy which demanded their mass action, their armed forces, battles and barricades. . . . This was an especially happy circumstance of our October Revolution, for which it is still being slandered as a military rising and almost a palace coup. It would be better if they asked: Did the Petrograd proletariat sympathize or did it not with the organizers of the October insurrection? . . . There are no two answers here. Yes, the Bolsheviks acted on the mandate of the Petrograd workers and soldiers.[92]

The months of advance and retreat, of revolutionary struggle, ended on October 25. Trotsky describes the situation the morning after the insurrection:

> Next morning I pounced upon the bourgeois and Menshevik-Populist papers. They had not even a word about the uprising. The newspapers had been making such a to-do about the coming action by armed soldiers, about the sacking, the inevitable rivers of blood, about an insurrection, that now they simply had failed to notice an uprising that was actually taking place. In the meantime, without confusion, without street-fights, almost without firing or bloodshed, one institution after another was being occupied by detachments of soldiers, sailors, and the Red Guards. . . .
>   . . . A delegation from the municipal Duma called to see me and asked me a few inimitable questions. "Do you propose military action? If so, what, and when?" The Duma would have to know of this "not less than twenty-four hours in advance." What measures had the Soviet taken to ensure safety and order? And so on, and so forth.
>   "Will you dissolve us for being opposed to the transfer of power to the Soviets?"

I replied: "The present Duma reflects yesterday: if a conflict arises, we will propose to the people that they elect a new Duma on the issue of power." The delegation left as it had come, but it had left behind it the feeling of an assured victory. Something had changed during the night. Three weeks ago we had gained a majority in the Petrograd Soviet. We were hardly more than a banner—with no printing-works, no funds, no branches. No longer ago than last night, the government ordered the arrest of the Military-Revolutionary Committee, and was engaged in tracing our address. Today a delegation from the city Duma comes to the 'arrested' Military-Revolutionary Committee to inquire about the fate of the Duma.[93]

Trotsky then describes a conversation he has with Lenin:

The power is taken over, at least in Petrograd. . . . Lenin . . . looks softly at me, with that sort of awkward shyness that with him indicates intimacy. "You know," he says hesitatingly, "from persecution and life underground, to come so suddenly into power. . . . " He pauses for the right word. "*Es schwindet* [it makes one giddy]," he concludes, changing suddenly into German, and circling his hand around his head. We look at each other and laugh a little. All this takes only a minute or two; then a simple "passing to next business."[94]

The promise of human emancipation was paramount in the minds of those who led the revolution. In one of his most moving passages, Lenin wrote:

Hitherto the whole creative genius of the human intellect has labored only to give the advantages of technique and civilization to the few, and to deprive the rest of the most elementary necessities—education and free development. But now all the marvels of technique, all the conquests of civilization, are the property of the whole people, and henceforth human intellect and genius will never be twisted into a means of oppression, a means of exploitation. We know this: surely it is worth striving with all our might to fulfill this stupendous historic task? The workers will carry out this titanic historic labor, for there are vast revolutionary powers slumbering in them, vast powers of renovation and regeneration.[95]

In a similar vein, Trotsky writes in his autobiography, *My Life:*

Marxism considers itself the conscious expression of the unconscious historical process. But the "unconscious process" in the historical-philosophical sense of the term—not in the psychological—coincides with its conscious expression only at its highest point when the masses, by sheer elemental pressure break through the social routine and give victorious expression to the deepest needs of historical development. And at such moments the highest theoretical consciousness of the epoch merges with the immediate action of those oppressed masses who are furthest away from theory. The creative union of the conscious with the unconscious is what one usually calls "inspiration." Revolution is the inspired frenzy of history.[96]

Rosa Luxemburg, who leveled some strong criticisms of the Bolsheviks, summed up the Russian Revolution's historical significance:

The Russian Revolution is the mightiest event of the World War. . . .

Whatever a party could offer of courage, revolutionary farsightedness and consistency in an historic hour, Lenin, Trotsky and the other comrades have given in good measure. All the revolutionary honor and capacity which western social democracy lacked were represented by the Bolsheviks. Their October uprising was not only the actual salvation of the Russian Revolution; it was also the salvation of the honor of international socialism. . . .

Everything that happens in Russia is comprehensible and represents an inevitable chain of causes and effects, the starting point and end term of which are: the failure of the German proletariat and the occupation of Russia by German imperialism. It would be demanding something superhuman from Lenin and his comrades if we should expect of them that under such circumstances they should conjure forth the finest democracy, the most exemplary dictatorship of the proletariat and a flourishing socialist economy. . . .

The danger begins only when they make a virtue of necessity forced upon them by these fatal circumstances . . . and want to recommend them to the international proletariat as a model of socialist tactics. . . .

What is in order is to distinguish the essential from the non-essential, the kernel from the accidental excrescences in the policies of the Bolsheviks. . . .

It is not a matter of this or that secondary question of tactics, but of the capacity for action of the proletariat, the strength to act, the will to power of socialism as such. In this, Lenin and Trotsky and their friends were the *first*, those who went ahead as an example to the proletariat of the world; they are still the *only ones* up to now who can cry with Hutten: "I have dared!"

This is the essential and *enduring* in Bolshevik policy. In *this* sense theirs is the immortal historical service of having marched at the head of the international proletariat with the conquest of political power and the practical placing of the problem of the realization of socialism, and having advanced mightily the settlement of the score between capital and labor in the entire world. In Russia the problem could only be posed. It could not be solved in Russia. And in *this* sense, the future everywhere belongs to "bolshevism."[97]

Today, we still need to fight for the "great awakening of the personality," as Trotsky put it. The day will come, not easily, not automatically, but it will come, when we can talk once more of "a great awakening of the personality" in the United States and internationally.

THE FALL OF STALINISM: TEN YEARS ON

ANTHONY ARNOVE

The collapse of Stalinism began ten years ago with mass demonstrations tearing down the Berlin Wall that had physically separated East and West Germany. From 1961 to 1989, East German security forces murdered more than 450 people trying to escape the East,[1] illustrating the distance between such "socialism" and the vision of a workers' democracy that had inspired the Russian Revolution in 1917.

By the end of 1991, Stalinist regimes that had seemed unshakable for decades were overthrown in East Germany, Poland, Hungary, Czechoslovakia, Romania, Bulgaria, Albania—and in the USSR itself, which then broke apart into fifteen new republics.

This was a tremendous victory for genuine socialism. But almost universally the opposite conclusion was drawn. Whether on the left or on the right, commentators treated 1989 and then 1991 as the "triumph of capitalism" and the "death of Marxism."

For the right, this was obviously a fact to be celebrated. The market and the West had won the battle against the "Evil Empire" and "eliminated any ideological alternative to free-market capitalism," in the words of *New York Times* columnist Thomas Friedman.[2] Republican president George Bush declared that the end of the Cold War represented the dawning of a "New World Order" of peace and global prosperity.[3] An obscure State Department official, Francis Fukuyama, became famous for arguing that we had reached "the end of history." Politics would no longer be defined by battles between socialism and capitalism; from now on, politics would revolve around how to tinker with capitalism.

Discussing what he termed "the ultimate victory of the VCR," Fukuyama declared that Western capitalism represented "the end point of mankind's ideological evolution" and the "final form of human government." We could now anticipate "accumulation without end."[4]

Several historians took the opportunity to argue that Stalinist barbarism was the inevitable outcome of any attempt to make revolutionary change. "The [Russian] experiment went horribly wrong, not so much because of the malice of its leaders, most of whom had started out with the highest ideals, but because their ideals were themselves impossible," concluded Orlando Figes in his post-fall revisionist history of the Russian Revolution, *A People's Tragedy*.[5]

Many on the left adopted a mirror image of this viewpoint. Capitalism had triumphed and socialism had been discredited. Revolutions inevitably lead to tyranny. Take the view of the Polish dissident leader Adam Michnik, for instance, who explains that "utopias lead to the guillotine and the gulag."[6]

Some quickly changed their colors and after years of defending the abuses of Stalinism, decided that the market was, after all, the best form of social organization of production we could achieve. The highly respected British historian and Communist Party member Eric Hobsbawm, who remained in the party after the Soviet repression of the Hungarian uprising of 1956, now proclaimed that Russia "obviously wasn't a workers' state." Indeed, he said, "nobody in the Soviet Union ever believed it was a workers' state, and the workers knew it wasn't a workers' state."[7]

Having decided that the Russian Revolution was a "freak accident," Hobsbawm wrote, "I agree with [the liberal economist] John Kenneth Galbraith that 'in a very real sense in both East and West our task is the same: it is to seek and find the system that combines the best in market-motivated and socially motivated action.'"[8] He adds that "the bad results of the market can be and have been to some extent controlled."[9]

Others, though, maintained their allegiances. For them, 1989 and 1991 represented a demoralizing defeat that left us with no other positive example of socialism.

Nation columnist Alexander Cockburn, one of the best writers on the American left, provided a clear example of this view.

> The Soviet Union defeated Hitler and fascism. Without it, the Cuban revolution would never have survived, nor the Vietnamese. In the postwar

years it was the counterweight to US imperialism and the terminal savageries of the old European colonial powers. It gave support to any country trying to follow an independent line.[10]

This was news, no doubt, to those who had tried to follow an independent line in Hungary, Czechoslovakia and Afghanistan.

What all of these views share is the completely mistaken belief that the totalitarian regimes of the Soviet Union and its satellites in Eastern Europe represented socialism and were heirs of some fashion to the tradition of Marxism.

This idea, however, turns Marxism and socialism on their heads.

Karl Marx and Frederick Engels wrote in *The Communist Manifesto:*

> The proletarian movement is the self-conscious, independent movement of the immense majority, in the interest of the immense majority. The proletariat . . . cannot stir, cannot raise itself up, without the whole superincumbent strata of official society being sprung up in the air.[11]

"The first step in the revolution by the working class," they added, "is to raise the proletariat to the position of ruling class, to win the battle for democracy. The proletariat will use its political supremacy to wrest, by degrees, all capital from the bourgeoisie, to centralise all instruments of production in the hands of the State, *i.e.*, of the proletariat organised as the ruling class."[12] The *Manifesto* concludes by describing socialism as a society without "classes and class antagonisms." In place of class society, "we shall have an association, in which the free development of each is the condition for the free development of all."[13]

Engels expressed the kernel of revolutionary socialism when he wrote that "the emancipation of the working class must be the act of the working class itself."[14] As Lenin later put the argument in *The State and Revolution*, "All previous revolutions perfected the state machine, whereas it must be broken, smashed."[15]

Yet Stalinism was actually the negation of socialism. It was the opposite of workers' control, democracy, a classless society and the smashing of the state.

The rise of Stalinism

Joseph Stalin came to power in Russia after the death of Lenin in 1924. Stalin—who had played so marginal a role in the Russian Revolution of 1917 that he would later ban John Reed's magnificent account, *Ten Days That Shook the World*, for revealing this fact—headed a counter-revolution that destroyed the gains and the promise of October.

Stalin's dictatorship arose from the defeat of the Russian Revolution and the failure of revolution to succeed in more advanced capitalist countries in Europe.

The Bolsheviks who led the October Revolution knew that a workers' state in an isolated and economically backward Russia could only survive if it spread and received material support for industrial development from economically advanced countries that had themselves made a workers' revolution.

The historian Moshe Lewin explains:

> In the eyes of its originators the October Revolution had neither meaning nor future independent of its international function as a catalyst and detonator: it was to be the first spark that would lead to the establishment of socialist regimes in countries which, unlike Russia, possessed an adequate economic infrastructure and cultural basis. Unless it fulfilled this function, the Soviet regime should not have even survived. Lenin often affirmed this belief, and persisted in this interpretation even after several years had elapsed without bringing any confirmation of his hopes.[16]

The possibility of the revolution spreading was not a utopian dream. The Belgian socialist Victor Serge captured the mood of the period: Riots in Paris, riots in Lyon, revolution in Belgium, revolution in Constantinople, victory of the soviets in Bulgaria, rioting in Copenhagen. In fact, the whole of Europe is in movement; clandestine or open Soviets are appearing everywhere, even in the Allied armies; everything is possible, everything."[17]

Millions around the world were inspired by the example of workers taking power in Russia. Yet, in country after country, the left failed to match the Bolsheviks' achievement in Russia. Most critically, the revolution in Germany was lost when the Social Democrats allied with the army officers and the industrialists to organize a counter-revolution that destroyed the German workers' councils and the Bavarian Soviet Republic.[18] At the same time, fourteen armies invaded Russia in an attempt to restore the old regime.[19] Russia faced a bloody and prolonged civil war that economically devastated the country.

The civil war in Russia lasted from 1918 to 1921. Russia was subjected to an imperialist blockade that cut off supplies and trade and was forced into battle on multiple fronts. Industrial and agricultural productivity dropped precipitously as resources were directed to fighting the invading armies and the forces of the old order, led by the White Army. "Production came to a standstill; the transport system totally collapsed; cities emptied; and social distinctions dropped to the denominator of extreme poverty. Famine and epidemic raged, and the barest essentials were lacking," the historian Michal Reiman notes in *The Birth of Stalinism*.[20]

By 1920, production had dropped to 18 percent of its 1913 level.[21] The population of Petrograd, the cradle of the Russian Revolution, fell from 2,400,000 in 1917 to 574,000 in August 1920.[22] The working class was literally being decimated. "The youngest and most energetic workers had gone to the front," notes Serge.[23]

Although the Bolsheviks emerged victorious from the war, the price was enormous, with more than seven million premature deaths. The Bolsheviks "paid for victory with the destruction of the proletariat that had made the revolution," writes Tony Cliff.[24] Without a working class and without production, workers' control of production was an impossibility, and the workers' state became unhinged from its social basis.

"Socialism in one country"

Stalinism represented a fundamental break from the Bolshevik tradition. In fact, Stalin had to drown the Bolshevik Party of 1917 in blood in order to consolidate his power and the victory of the bureaucracy.

Stalin's project can be summed up in the phrase he first used in the fall of 1924: "Socialism in one country."[25] This concept broke with one of the central ideas of Marxism—that socialism could not exist in isolation, given that capitalism was a global system. Under conditions of famine, economic and military collapse, political isolation and the devastation of the Russian working class, Stalinism sought to achieve "socialism" through rapid industrialization directed by a dictatorship of the bureaucracy that took over the Communist Party.

This led to brutality on an immense scale. In essence, Stalin embarked on what Marx had called "primitive accumulation," the earliest and bloodiest stage of the development of capitalism, when as Marx put it,

"Capital comes dripping from head to toe, from every pore, with blood and dirt."[26]

But Stalin sought to do in five years what England had done in more than one hundred. Stalin's first "five-year plan," announced in 1928, set the pace for rapid industrialization on the backs of Russian workers, with ever higher and more inhumane targets. In January 1932, Commissar of Heavy Industry G. K. Ordzhonikidze proclaimed:

In the course of one year we must more than double the capacity of the metal factories. . . . How much time did it take the countries of capitalism to achieve the same thing? . . . England took thirty-five years to accomplish this. . . . It took Germany ten years . . . [and] the United States eight years. The USSR must cover the same ground in one year.[27]

This method of accumulation for competition with "the countries of capitalism" was achieved through the enormous exploitation of the working class, as well as the peasantry, which was subjected to forced collectivization of farming. Millions of Russians starved, while another ten million labored in the gulag, Stalin's prison-labor system.[28]

The Communist Party, now the organization of the ruling bureaucracy, the *nomenklatura*, directed and controlled every aspect of the society. Planning did not exist to meet human need, but to accumulate. A command economy with a bureaucratic "plan" strictly subordinated agriculture, consumer goods and the wages of the working class to heavy industry and armaments. Any dissent was brutally suppressed by Stalin's security forces, who wiped out the soviets (workers' councils), workers' control over production, trade unions and every vestige of workers' power won by the working class in the October Revolution.

To those who argued that Stalin's terror grew naturally out of the Russian Revolution and the Bolsheviks' program, the revolutionary leader Leon Trotsky pointed out that it was necessary for Stalin to liquidate the Bolshevik leadership of 1917 and systematically restructure the party to achieve his aims:

The unimpeachable language of figures mercilessly refutes the assertion so current among the democratic intellectuals that Stalinism and Bolshevism are "one and the same." Stalinism originated not as an organic growth out of Bolshevism but as a negation of Bolshevism consummated in blood. The program of this negation is mirrored very graphically in the history of the Central Committee. Stalinism had to exterminate first politically and then physically the leading cadres of Bolshevism in order to become what it now is: an apparatus of the privileged, a brake upon historical progress, an agency of world imperialism. Stalinism and Bolshevism are mortal enemies.[29]

Trotsky noted in 1939 that of the twenty-one members of the Bolshevik Central Committee of 1917, "only one remains at the present time in the party leadership—Stalin." Seven were "shot or condemned to the firing squad . . . three have disappeared during the purges; three others have been liquidated politically—and perhaps physically: a total of thirteen . . . turned out to be 'enemies of the people.'"[30]

Trotsky's own case illustrates the pattern. A leader of the revolution and then of the Red Army during the civil war, Trotsky was forced into physical exile and later murdered by Stalin's agents in Mexico in 1940.

It was from the ranks of the Bolshevik Party that the opposition to the rise of the Stalinist bureaucracy came, while capitalist politicians in the West hailed Stalin as a rejection of revolutionary internationalism and a "return to realism." Stalin was seen as someone with whom deals could be cut. The struggle to maintain workers' democracy and socialist internationalism against the Stalinist counter-revolution was organized by Trotsky and the Bolshevik Left Opposition, whose efforts kept alive the ideas of Marxism to be passed on to a new generation of revolutionary fighters.

State capitalism in Russia

Developing the ideas of Leon Trotsky, the Palestinian socialist Tony Cliff argued in 1947 that the first five-year plan represented a reintroduction of capitalism in Russia.[31] Cliff said that the Soviet Union could best be understood as bureaucratic state capitalism.[32]

The October Revolution had "raise[d] the proletariat to the position of ruling class."[33] In Trotsky's phrase, the revolution represented "the forcible entrance of the masses into the realm of rulership over their own destiny."[34]

Yet, under Stalin, the state owned the means of production, but the workers did not own the state. Workers had no control over their lives, production or the government, despite all the lofty phrases of Stalin's apologists. In Russia, the Communist Party bureaucracy controlled the state and state property and collectively occupied the role of the exploiting class.

Before 1928, production in Russia remained subordinated to meeting consumption needs. Despite the conditions imposed by isolation and civil war, Serge observed "queues of fifty to a hundred people [who] stand outside the bakeries where the commune distributes to everybody the bread it has available."[35]

This radically changed with the introduction of the five-year plan in 1928. "From then on accumulation leaped ahead tremendously, while the standard of living of the masses not only lagged far behind, but even declined absolutely compared with 1928."[36]

Each plan was increasingly oriented to the production of further means of production, rather than to meeting the needs of Russian workers, whose standard of living declined even as their productivity increased. Real wages dropped 50 percent between 1928 and 1936, while labor productivity more than tripled.[37] During the same period, more than five million Russians were driven into forced labor.[38] Meanwhile, the ruling bureaucratic class composed of factory managers, military officers and state and party officials lived in the luxury that comes with class power and privilege. Of urban homes built in 1935, one-third had no water supply, 38 percent had no sewage system and 55 percent had no heating system. In 1938, munitions plants consumed 94 percent of Russian iron and steel production.[39]

Under capitalism, Marx and Engels wrote in *The Communist Manifesto*, "living labour is but a means to increase accumulated labor." Under socialism, however, "accumulated labour is but a means to widen, to enrich, to promote the existence of the labourer."[40]

In a world capitalist system, Russia was forced to compete economically and militarily with the Western powers. Stalinism set out to compete with the capitalist superpowers on their terms.

The spread of Stalinism

Stalinism not only buried the Russian Revolution; with tragic results, it became a model for other revolutionaries internationally. The Stalinists covered themselves with the prestige of the Russian Revolution, which had inspired millions looking for an alternative to capitalist war, oppression and exploitation. Around the world, Communist Parties equated Russia with socialism and covered up—or justified—each new abuse of the bureaucracy.

"Socialism in one country" came to mean socialism nowhere else, as the Stalinist bureaucracy viewed working-class revolution as a threat to its class privileges and rule. The Stalinists' influence directly contributed to the failure of the 1925–27 Chinese revolution, the defeat of the proletariat in the Spanish Civil War and the muting of class struggle in numerous countries where the Communist Party exerted influence, notably in Italy, France and the United States. In the early 1930s, the German Communist Party (KPD) viewed the Social Democrats as a greater evil than the Nazis. The KPD's failure to unite with social democrats to smash Hitler counts among Stalinism's greatest crimes. In the 1960s, the Indonesian Communist Party supported an alliance with Sukarno and the military, which eventually turned on them and slaughtered as many as one million workers and peasants. During the presidency of Salvador Allende in Chile, the Communist Party was a proponent of the parliamentary road, opposed the workers' *cordones* (councils) and preached alliance with General Augusto Pinochet and the military until they destroyed the Chilean revolution. Similarly, the Communist Party fought for an alliance with the existing state and army in the 1974–75 Portuguese Revolution.

Communist Parties systematically subordinated the interests of the working class to Russia's changing foreign policy line. To paraphrase Trotsky, they were transformed from revolutionary vanguards into Stalin's border guards.[41] But building on the prestige of the Russian Revolution, they were often able to organize the more militant section of the working class, thus creating a massive obstacle to the building of genuine revolutionary socialist parties.

As Cliff explains, it was precisely the failures and weaknesses of the left that strengthened the appeal of the Stalinist model.

There have been strong links binding the international Communist movement to Moscow. For a long time it suffered one setback after another: in Germany over and over again from the defeat of the revolution in 1918 to the rise of Hitler; in China the defeat of the 1925–27 revolution; the defeat of the Republic in the Spanish Civil War; the debacle of the People's Front in France, etc., etc. The only Communist Party maintaining power was that in Russia. "If man's weakness in [the] face of the forces of nature or society lead[s] to his imbibing the opiate of religion with its promise of a better world to come, Stalinism certainly became the opiate of the international labour movement during the long period of suffering and impotence."[42]

Despite the criminal role the Stalinists played in allowing the rise of Hitler, including the signing of a pact with him, Russia gained even more prestige from its military defeat of Germany at the end of the Second World War.[43]

In addition, Stalinism could claim success as it expanded its reach to what became known as its "satellite states." Russia had already annexed Lithuania, Latvia, Estonia and Eastern Poland and incorporated a number of previously autonomous republics. Then, at the end of the war, the Great Powers divided up Europe amongst themselves. Poland, Eastern Germany, Czechoslovakia, Hungary, Yugoslavia, Romania and Bulgaria were carved out by Stalin.[44]

In none of these cases had workers mounted a revolution or the working class taken power. As Cliff wrote in 1952, "The 'People's Democracies' are based on a different conception. A bureaucratic police dictatorship has raised itself above the people, and is independent of its will, while claiming to govern in its interests."[45]

Various socialists in the West came up with confusing assessments of what these regimes represented, but many saw them as some form of socialism or state preferable to capitalism. Marx and Engels must have been wrong, therefore, to believe that "the emancipation of the working class must be the act of the working class itself." Socialism could now be imposed at gunpoint by the Russian Army.

In the minds of millions, socialism no longer meant workers' power but nationalized property. The equation "state ownership equals socialism" was a complete departure from the Marxist tradition. In *Anti-Dühring*, Engels polemicized against the idea that "*every* statification . . . is socialistic." If "statification" equals socialism, he reasoned, "then Napoleon and Metternich are to be counted among the founders of socialism" for nationalizing tobacco production.[46]

The key to understanding a society is not the abstract form of property, but the actual class relations defining the social relations of production. In Russia under Stalin, the working class was subjected to capitalist exploitation and discipline; accumulation and competition drove production, not need.

Those who looked to the Stalinist model of development, however, cast Marxism aside. Instead, they argued that the "Communist world" would soon economically outstrip the West, "proving" its superiority to capitalism by creating faster growth rates and a higher standard of living.

Other leftists, rightly reacting to Stalin's crimes at home and abroad, flipped this view on its head and decided that Stalinism was so evil that it was necessary to defend Western capitalism as an alternative. This confusion led a generation of former radicals and revolutionaries to become jingoistic supporters of U.S. imperialism during the Cold War.[47]

This is why Cliff's analysis of state capitalism would prove to be so decisive.

Neither Washington nor Moscow

Cliff's theory of state capitalism maintained the revolutionary tradition of socialism from below when socialism had come to be identified with Stalinism—or, alternatively, with social-democratic governments in Europe, such as Britain's Labor Party, that merely sought to manage the capitalist system and also identified socialism with control of the "state sector." The theory of state capitalism sustained a generation of activists whose slogan "neither Washington nor Moscow" rejected both of the two main poles of imperialism internationally. It also showed that the USSR and its satellite states were not immune from the contradictions that all capitalist countries face: economic crisis and working-class struggle.

While Stalin's apologists claimed that the working class was in power in Russia and Western defenders claimed that the working class had no hope for struggle against such a brutal regime, those in the International Socialist (IS) tendency founded by Cliff always had confidence that workers could bring down the Stalinist regimes through their own activity.

As early as 1948, Cliff wrote in a chapter called "The Class Struggle in Russia":

> In order to raise the productivity of labour above a certain point, the standard of living of the masses must rise, as workers who are undernourished, badly housed and uneducated are not capable of modern production. . . . But workers, besides having hands, have heads. The raising of the standard of living and culture of the masses means raising their self-confidence, increasing their appetite, their impatience at the lack of democratic rights and personal security, and their impatience [with] the bureaucracy which preserves these burdens. On the other hand, not to raise the standard of living of the masses means to perpetuate the low productivity of labor which would be fatal for the bureaucracy in

the present international situation, and would tend to drive the masses sooner or later to revolts of despair...[T]he bureaucracy is bringing into being a force which will sooner or later clash violently with it.[48]

Stalinist industrialization, while immiserating millions, also created a large industrial working class. Indeed, the working class revolted throughout decades of Stalinism, notably in East Germany in 1953, Hungary and Poland in 1956, Czechoslovakia in 1968 and Poland in 1980–81.[49]

In 1989, the contradictions that Cliff described could no longer be contained by the ruling classes. The countries of the Soviet Empire, especially Russia, were experiencing serious economic crisis and growing difficulties maintaining their legitimacy.

Rather than outstripping and defeating capitalism, the more privatized and market-driven form of capitalism in the West outpaced the bureaucratized, state-dominated capitalism of Russia and its satellites. As Cliff points out, "In the first five-year plan the annual rate of growth of the [Russian] economy was 19.2 percent. In the period 1950–59 it was 5.8 percent. In the 1970s the growth rate was 3.7 percent annually. And then it went down to 1 percent [in the 1980s]."[50]

The economic stagnation, the drudgery and alienation of work, the stifling of culture and intellectual life by the bureaucracy and the harshness of living conditions produced a popular desire for change. When the dam began to break, the workers did not defend the "workers' states" because there was nothing that was theirs to defend.

The collapse

In the mid-1980s, elements of the Stalinist bureaucracy recognized that they could not maintain control, overcome crisis or compete effectively with Western capitalism without offering some reforms. In 1986, Russian prime minister Mikhail Gorbachev launched a program of *perestroika* (restructuring) and *glasnost* (openness). Thousands took advantage of the new cracks in the Stalinist edifice to express their desire for change.

In 1988 and 1989, strikes and illegal rallies took place in Russia, Hungary, East Germany and elsewhere. Ten thousand people held an illegal demonstration in March 1988 in Hungary, demanding "democracy, free speech and freedom of the press."[51] During the same period, Russia was confronted with nationalist movements in Latvia, Estonia,

Lithuania, Uzbekistan and several other republics.[52] As one East German recalled ten years later, "A feeling arose that things had to change."[53]

In the summer of 1989, when Hungary opened its borders, thousands of East German refugees crossed to escape to the West. On October 18, East German hard-liner Erich Honecker, who had ruled in East Germany since 1971, was pushed out of office. When his replacement, Egon Krenz, visited Gorbachev in Moscow on October 31, Gorbachev indicated that he was opposed to reunification of East and West Germany, but that he would not back the use of force to contain the flow of refugees from the East. On the evening of November 9, when protesters gathered at the Berlin Wall and demanded to be allowed across, the leadership buckled. Several protesters were allowed across, and then the dam broke.[54]

When they sensed that repression alone could not contain the crisis, the Stalinist bureaucracies faced a decision: be pushed or jump. In the end, both took place. Under the pressure of protests, strikes and demonstrations, the regimes fell one by one.

Millions took to the streets to express their desire for change, but only in Romania was violence used in any significant way, when the hated dictator Nicolae Ceausescu and his wife were executed on Christmas in 1989. Two hundred thousand people demonstrated in Prague on November 20, 1989.[55] The protests grew to include broad sections of workers who joined strikes to bring down the government.[56] Within days, the number in the streets had soared to as many as 800,000 calling for a fundamental change. On November 27, millions walked out of work for a two-hour general strike.[57]

Protests spread like wildfire. An East German socialist described the mood of the time: "In the first few months after the revolution everything seemed to have changed. We were seized with the idea of being able to change everything. People became more confident. Ordinary people spoke at demonstrations and meetings. We won the right to travel, freedom of opinion and . . . the right to strike."[58]

"Shock therapy"

The expectations for change were bound to come up against the limitation of the changes taking place in Eastern Europe. We should not underestimate the significance of the revolutions that took place; but, in reality, the same managers ran the plants the next day, the same police officers and security forces remained intact, and yesterday's Communist *apparatchik* became today's "democrat," "free marketeer" or "reformer."

If those who thought the Soviet Union and its satellites were socialist were right, then how could capitalism have replaced socialism almost overnight without any radical restructuring of the way production was organized and with only minor changes to the names and titles within the ruling class?

What happened was actually a step sideways. It was not a transition from socialism to capitalism, but a restructuring of capitalism, similar in fact to the kind of restructuring the International Monetary Fund and the World Bank have overseen in Bolivia, Brazil and other countries.[59]

Though some in the bureaucracy tried to cling to the same ways of ruling, the more forward-looking elements of the ruling class realized that it was no longer possible to survive using the old means of control. They sought to preserve—and actually, in many ways, to extend—their power and privileges through opening up to and cooperating with multinational capitalism.

Even before the collapse, one Hungarian sociologist remarked in 1988:

> It is not unusual today to meet a family belonging to the Kadariste oligarchy where the father is a high-ranking party or state official, the daughter owns a town centre clothes shop, the eldest son represents a Western company in Hungary, the son-in-law is the chairman of a recently created company or a Western bank and a grandmother owns a family hotel on the edge of Lake Balaton.[60]

In Poland, a recent study of the former Stalinist *nomenklatura* found that one-quarter had set up their own firms or held high-ranking jobs in private companies, 15 to 20 percent held high-ranking jobs in state companies and 15 percent received special high-paying pensions.[61]

The new ruling classes in Eastern Europe—though headed by dissidents such as Lech Walesa, who had led the working-class Solidarity movement in Poland—saw their task as encouraging "enterprise" and competition. In fact, they oversaw the imposition of harsh austerity measures, called "shock therapy," in order to compete more effectively with other capitalist countries. Sacrifice for a short time, workers were told, and you will soon be rewarded.

But the promises that politicians made for the market and the New World Order all turned out to be false. "I thought there would be a very difficult transition lasting three years, five years, seven years," the Russian politician Anatoly Chubais said recently. "Now it is clear that it will take decades."[62]

Like everywhere else that capitalism has been restructured, this process has had a devastating impact on the working class. While they have gained important freedoms, workers have faced repeated rounds of cuts in social spending, growing unemployment and privatization. Contrary to all the triumphalist rhetoric about how the market would bring happiness and a Western standard of living to the former Communist countries, most people's standard of living actually took a step backward. Poland, East Germany and the Czech Republic, which split from its poorer partner Slovakia in 1993, have seen growth and wage improvements, but they have also seen unemployment rise to unprecedented levels. East German unemployment now stands at 20 percent. In Poland, the *New York Times* reported, "the zloty has fallen by about 15 percent this year, a once high-flying stock market has been pummeled, unemployment is now over 10 percent, fuel prices are rising, and anger over layoffs in loss-making heavy industries like steel and coal has boiled over."[63]

The *Economist* magazine now glibly admits:

Heading west has not brought instant contentment. Far from it. . . . It has been a rough decade. The euphoria of political freedom wore off quickly as the pain of economic reform began to bite. . . . The very workers—ship-builders and miners, for instance—who have done so much to bring down communism were often the first to lose their jobs in the brave new world. . . . The gap between the haves and have-nots is widening. . . . In almost every ex-communist country, standards of health care have plunged. In some, lives have suddenly grown shorter.[64]

From 1987 to 1997, life expectancy declined in Romania, Albania, Bulgaria, Russia and the Ukraine.[65]

According to new World Bank figures, "In Eastern Europe and the former Soviet Union . . . the number of people who are living under the poverty line of $4 a day has grown, from 14 million in 1989 to 147 million today."[66]

In 1997, the *New York Times* reported:

Russian men are dying in middle age at a rate unparalleled in modern history. . . . Per capita alcohol consumption is the highest in the world. . . . A wider gap has developed in life expectancy between men (59) and women

(73) than in any other country. . . . The death rate among working-age Russians today is higher than a century ago. . . . The raw number of sick children, appallingly high by any standard, appears lower this year only because so few children have been born over the past several years. . . . The Russian population fell by 480,000 last year, the steepest such decline in any year since World War II.[67]

The situation is worse in nonurban areas. In Dzerzhinsk, which is only 250 miles east of Moscow, "life expectancy is just 42 years for men, 47 for women. Serfs breaking rocks in the Czar's Russia lived longer than that."[68]

The story is brutal—but it is a version of the same story of what capitalism looks like today around the globe.[69] In Tanzania, for example, "one in six children dies before the age of five, and almost one-third of the population will not live until 40. Yet . . . [in 1998], more than one-third of the budget will go to external debt servicing. On a per capita basis . . . this means that Tanzania has been spending nine times as much on debt servicing as on basic health."[70]

Ten years after

The year 1989 did not mark the dawn of a new world order of peace and prosperity. Instead, it was the beginning of a period that has seen the 1991 Gulf War and the ongoing war against Iraq, where sanctions have led to hundreds of thousands of Iraqi deaths; the economic crisis in the former Soviet republics and Yugoslavia, in which nationalist leaders like Franjo Tuđjman in Croatia and Slobodan Milošević in Serbia sought to preserve their power by whipping up ethnic nationalism and provoking ethnic cleansing on a mass scale; NATO's brutal war on Yugoslavia to extend the power and influence of the United States and the other NATO powers; and an international arms-spending and nuclear-weapons race.

These events have thoroughly disoriented much of the left. It was, after all, governments of the left, even ones calling themselves "socialist," that cheered NATO's assault in the Balkans the most vociferously and pushed hardest for a ground war.

The editors of *Dissent*, the journal of the Democratic Socialists of America, now celebrate their own political confusion and retreats. In a featured contribution to a special issue, "Ten Years After the Fall," editorial board member Paul Berman writes:

Universally despised phrases like "the third way" sound bracing and attractive, in my ears, because, at least, they imply a turn against the assumptions of the past . . .

Every left-wing discussion from now on should begin with the question. . . . What do we actively support today that would have provoked our indignation yesterday?[71]

In the same forum, the Polish dissident Adam Michnik praises Ronald Reagan, whose "description of the 'Evil Empire' gave strength and courage to the people fighting for freedom against Communist dictatorships," and explains that "the idea of worker self-government—an effective instrument in the struggle against the communist *nomenklatura*—turned out to be completely useless under the conditions of a market economy."[72]

All too often today, debates on the left are not about how we can change society, but whether it is even possible or desirable to change it. In part, this is because of the political vacuum left by the collapse of Stalinism. The Communist Parties internationally attracted the best fighters in the working class, despite having politics that drove workers' militancy into the dead end of Stalinism.

Rarely, if ever, has there been such a gap between the need for a revolutionary alternative and the level of organization of the left as exists today on an international level. Around the world, we see mounting evidence of the failures of capitalism—more misery, greater polarization of wealth and life expectations and wars that are claiming millions of lives. The economic crisis now affecting more than one-third of the world economy has exposed even more sharply the madness of a market system that means people go hungry because too many goods have been produced to sell profitably on the market.

Nowhere is this gap greater than in the former state capitalist countries, where many workers express the feeling that they have "tried socialism" and know that it didn't work. With the resurgence of anti-Semitic, ultranationalist and Stalinist politicians taking advantage of popular disillusionment with the failure of the market to deliver for ordinary people, the need to provide an alternative that can explain why state capitalism was not socialism couldn't be more urgent.

History "weighs like a nightmare on the brain of the living," Marx wrote in *The Eighteenth Brumaire of Louis Bonaparte*.[73] The weight of Stalinism was massive. Chris Harman writes:

One idea dominated the thinking of the left throughout the world for half a century—the idea that socialist countries already existed. It is an idea which has . . . paralysed those who would fight for a better society. They have seen the so-called socialist countries reproduce all the evils of the capitalist society they were supposed to replace.

There have been economic crises driving millions to desperation (Poland), the wholesale sacking of workers and the formation of "reserve armies" of the unemployed (Yugoslavia and China), the use of tanks to conquer other peoples (Hungary, Czechoslovakia, Afghanistan), border wars between "socialist armies" (Russia and China, China and Vietnam), state incitement of anti-Semitism (Poland), the mass deployment of slave labour (Stalin's Russia), even the establishment of extermination camps (Kampuchea [Cambodia]). The accumulation of wealth has continued to be accompanied by the accumulation of poverty, massive privileges by massive drudgery, the promise of liberation by the reality of repression.

For a whole generation the great majority of socialists in the West and the third world tried to ignore these realities. They tried to defend the indefensible, to hide from themselves what they could not hide from others, to cover up for their own uncertainty by empty rhetoric.

Even when the illusions in Russia died in the 1960s, a new generation frequently substituted illusions in China, Cuba, Vietnam or Kampuchea. But to no avail. Time and again real historical developments caught them unawares, leaving them without arguments as successive leaders pointed to the crime of their predecessors, as the rulers of one "socialist" state poured abuse upon the rulers of another.[74]

The collapse of these illusions opened a new act in history, but it has not done away with the weight of the past. The Polish socialist Daniel Singer captures this contradiction in his book, *Whose Millennium? Theirs or Ours?*

> We are at a moment, to borrow [Walt] Whitman's words, when society "is for a while between things ended and things begun," not because of some symbolic date on a calendar marking the turn of the millennium, but because the old order is a-dying, in so far as it can no longer provide answers corresponding to the social needs of our point of development, though it clings successfully to power, because there is no class, no social force ready to push it off the historical stage.[75]

Socialism from below

The events of 1989 provide a historic opportunity for socialists to reclaim the genuine tradition of socialism from below—the tradition of Karl Marx, Frederick Engels, Rosa Luxemburg, V. I. Lenin, Leon Trotsky and Antonio Gramsci.[76]

Around the world, workers are fighting against the devastating impact of the market on their lives. The collapse of Stalinism means that those workers can make their way to the only tradition capable of explaining the crisis of capitalism and the fall of Stalinism and providing a real alternative: workers' democratic control from below; production for human need, not profit; and international socialism.

The twentieth century has seen terrible crimes: the gulags of Stalin, the death camps of Hitler, the Vietnam War and Hiroshima and Nagasaki. All were expressions of capitalism.

But the twentieth century has also seen the massive growth of the force that can put an end to such barbarism—the international working class, the group that has the power to end capitalism with its "classes and class antagonisms" and replace it with a society "in which the free development of each is the condition for the free development of all."

THE RUSSIAN REVOLUTION
FURTHER READING

Tony Cliff, Duncan Hallas, Chris Harman and Leon Trotsky,
   Party and Class
Tony Cliff, *Lenin: Building the Party*
Tony Cliff, *Lenin: All Power to the Soviets*
Tony Cliff, *Lenin: Revolution Besieged*
Tony Cliff, *Leon Trotsky: Towards October, 1879–1917*
Tony Cliff, *Leon Trotsky: The Sword of the Revolution, 1917–1923*
Tony Cliff, *Leon Trotsky: Fighting the Rising Stalinist Bureaucracy,
   1923–1927*
Tony Cliff, *Leon Trotsky: The Darker the Night the Brighter the Star,
   1927–1940*
Alexander Rabinowitch, *The Bolsheviks Come to Power*
John Reed, *Ten Days That Shook the World*
John Rees, *In Defense of October*
Alfred Rosmer, *Lenin's Moscow*
Victor Serge, *Year One of the Russian Revolution*
Leon Trotsky, *The History of the Russian Revolution*
Leon Trotsky, *The Lessons of October*

NOTES

Chapter 1: WORKERS' REVOLUTION AND BEYOND

1. V Lenin, *Collected Works* translated from the fourth Russian edition, volume 26, pages 470–1.
2. Lenin, volume 27, page 98.
3. T Cliff, *State Capitalism in Russia* (London 1974) pages 283–5.
4. K Marx, *Capital*, volume 1 (Harmondsworth 1976) page 742.

Chapter 2: HOW THE REVOLUTION WAS LOST

1. Leon Trotsky, *History of the Russian Revolution* (London 1965) page 72.
2. Martov to Axelrod, 19 November 1917, quoted by Israel Getzler, *Martov* (Cambridge 1967).
3. Getzler, page 183.
4. Getzler, page 199.
5. See Trotsky, *Hue and Cry over Kronstadt*.
6. Quoted by Max Schachtman, *The Struggle for the New Course* (New York 1943) page 150.
7. Lenin, volume 32, page 24.
8. See Lenin's response to Riazanov's demand that the habit of different groups within the party putting forward 'platforms' be prohibited: 'We cannot deprive the party and the members of the central committee of the right to appeal to the party in the event of disagreement on fundamental issues. I cannot imagine how we can do such a thing!' (Lenin, volume 32, page 261).
9. Appendix to E H Carr, *The Interregnum*, page 369.
10. Quoted in Schachtman, page 172.
11. Carr, page 39.
12. Carr, page 39.
13. Compare Stalin, *Lenin and Leninism* (Russian edition 1924) page 40: 'Can the final victory of socialism in one country be attained without the joint efforts of the proletarians of several advanced countries? No, this is impossible.' (Cited by Trotsky, *The Third International after Lenin*, page 36).

14.   We do not deal here with the early oppositions, for example the Workers' Opposition and the Democratic Centralists. Although these arose as a response to the early bureaucratisation and degeneration of the revolution, they were also partly a utopian reaction against objective reality as such (for example, the real strength of the peasants and the real weakness of the working class). What survived and mattered in the Workers' Opposition eventually became part of the Left Opposition, while its leaders, Kollontai and Shlyapnikov, capitulated to Stalin.

Chapter 3: THE NATURE OF STALINIST RUSSIA AND THE EASTERN BLOC

1.   Martov to Axelrod, 19 November 1917, quoted in Getzler.
2.   Trotsky, *History of the Russian Revolution*, page 812.
3.   S M Schwartz, quoted in Schachtman, *The Bureaucratic Revolution* (New York 1962) page 69.
4.   Trotsky, *History*, page 55.
5.   For details see the previous chapter. Also Tony Cliff, 'Trotsky on Substitutionism' in *International Socialism*, first series, number 2.
6.   Trotsky, *History*, page 1147.
7.   Lenin, quoted in Moshe Lewin, *Lenin's Last Struggle* (London 1969) page 12.
8.   Over the question of Georgia, see Lewin, pages 91 and following.
9.   Schwartz, quoted in Schachtman, *The Bureaucratic Revolution*.
10.   For fuller information on this whole section see Tony Cliff, *Russia: A Marxist Analysis* (London, no date) chapter 1. This book was later republished as *State Capitalism in Russia* (London 1974).
11.   For a fuller account of wage bargaining in these years, see E H Carr and R W Davies, *Foundations of a Planned Economy*, volume 1 (London 1969) chapter 19.
12.   See one estimate in Cliff, page 36.
13.   See Carr and Davies, Sections A and B; also I Deutscher, *Stalin* (London 1961) pages 328 and following.
14.   Carr and Davies, page 563.
15.   Regulations quoted in Cliff, page 25.
16.   For estimates, see Cliff. For a differing estimate for the years 1928–33, see Carr and Davies, page 342.
17.   Cliff, pages 30–1.
18.   Carr and Davies, page xii.
19.   Carr and Davies, page 277.
20.   Kuibishev, quoted in Carr and Davies, page 295.
21.   Kuibishev, quoted in Carr and Davies, page 313.
22.   Compare Cliff, page 33.
23.   Stalin, *Problems of Leninism*, page 356, quoted in Deutscher, page 328.
24.   Stalin, quoted in Carr and Davies, page 327.
25.   Marx, *Capital*, volume 1, pages 648–652.

26. Although Engels writes quite clearly: 'until 1865 the stock exchange was still a *secondary* element in the capitalist system' (Afterword to Marx's *Capital*, volume 3, page 884).

27. For such an identification, see Ernest Mandel, *The Inconsistencies of State Capitalism* (London 1969).

28. Again, see Mandel.

29. Marx, *Fondements de la Critique de l'économie politique* (Paris 1967) page 147.

30. Marx, *Fondements de la Critique de l'économie politique*, page 147.

31. Marx, *Capital*, volume 1, page 592.

32. Marx, *Capital*, volume 1, page 592.

33. Rudolf Hilferding, *Das Finanzkapital* (Vienna 1910) page 286.

34. Lenin, *Works* (in Russian), volume 35, page 51, quoted in Cliff, page 153.

35. Trade between the USSR and the West, although increasing, accounts for only about 1 per cent of total Russian production [in 1971—editor's note]. This has, however, been of decisive importance at certain points in Russian developments. For instance, the drop in the price of agricultural produce on the world market in the early 1930s forced Stalin to sell much greater quantities abroad in order to buy machinery needed for industrialisation, and therefore to extract a much greater surplus through 'collectivisation' than would otherwise have been the case. With some other Stalinist states the direct pressure of trade competition has been greater—for example Czechoslovakia and Cuba.

36. Marx, *The 1844 Manuscripts* (Moscow 1959) page 70.

37. In the early 1930s Stalin seems to have needed the personnel of the various oppositions insofar as he lacked capable, educated manpower. It was not until after 1930 that these began to be produced by the Stalinised education system. But between 1928 and 1940 the number of specialists increased 77-fold. This made it possible for Stalin to eliminate physically some of his opponents and make others politically impotent.

38. Above all by Trotsky.

39. Also in North Korea, but not in Yugoslavia and Albania, where the regimes resulted from purely indigenous movements.

40. See, for example, Harrison Salisbury, *The Coming War Between Russia and China* (London 1969), or for a much earlier account Ygael Gluckstein's *Mao's China* (London 1957) pages 394 and following, and for Yugoslavia, Milovan Djilas, *Conversations with Stalin* (London 1967) pages 11–14.

41. Many supporters of Trotsky who took seriously his definition of the Stalinist parties as 'counter-revolutionary.'

42. Even at world-market prices less-developed countries are exploited by more developed ones. See, for instance, Popovic, *On Economic Relations between Socialist Countries* (London 1950).

43. Berba, quoted in Ygael Gluckstein, *Stalin's Satellites in Europe* (London 1952) page 245. For further details, see Hal Draper, 'The Economic Drive behind Tito,' in *New International*, October 1948, and A Sayer, 'Between East and West,' in *International Socialism*, first series, number 41.

44. *Peking Review*, 8 May 1964. Marxists in the West had been aware of this exploitative relationship long before—see Gluckstein, page 167.

45. Financy, SSR 28/69.

46. For the best account of this period see Jacek Kuron and Karol Modzelewski, *A Revolutionary Socialist Manifesto (An Open Letter to the Party)* (London 1967) published as *Solidarność: The Missing Link?* (London 1982). For documents from 1956 to 1957, see *Pologne-Hongrie*, 1956, edited by J. J. Marie and B. Nagy (Paris 1966).

47. For example, the 'virgin lands scheme' and the organisation of industry through Sovnarkhozy.

48. The only one to refuse to confess, Krestinsky, relented under pressure.

49. Kuron and Modzelewski, page 54.

50. For a much longer account of Trotsky's analysis, see Cliff, *State Capitalism in Russia*.

51. Trotsky, *The Workers' Slate and the Question of Thermidor and Bonapartism* (London, no date) page 8.

52. Trotsky, *The Revolution Betrayed* (London 1957) page 59.

53. Trotsky, *The Workers' State and the Question of Thermidor and Bonapartism*, page 19.

54. Trotsky, *The Revolution Betrayed*.

55. Trotsky, *The Class Nature of the Soviet State* (London 1967) page 13.

56. Trotsky, *The Workers' State and the Question of Thermidor and Bonapartism*, page 4.

57. Trotsky, *The Revolution Betrayed*, page 235.

58. Trotsky, *Problems of Development in the USSR* (New York 1931) page 36.

59. Trotsky, *The Revolution Betrayed*, page 249.

60. Trotsky, *The Revolution Betrayed*, page 249.

61. Trotsky, *The USSR and the War*.

Chapter 4: THE THEORY OF STATE CAPITALISM

1. See the accompanying essay in this volume, Chris Harman's 'How the Revolution was Lost.'

2. *The Economist*, 5 April 1986, page 19.

3. See *Keesings Contemporary Archives*, 1982, page 31780.

4. CPSU Central Committee Resolution, September 1929; quoted in Cliff, *State Capitalism in Russia*, page 13.

5. Cliff, *State Capitalism in Russia*, page 23.

6. Tony Cliff, *Russia: A Marxist Analysis* (London 1965) page 31.

7. Victor Serge, *From Lenin to Stalin* (New York 1973) page 68. The quotation is from 1933.

8. Cliff, *Russia: A Marxist Analysis*, page 286.

9. *Pravda*, 22 December 1947, quoted in Cliff, *State Capitalism in Russia*, page 109.

10. Marx, *Capital* volume 1 (Moscow edition) pages 751–53.

11. Marx, *Capital* volume 1, page 751.

12. Marx, *Grundrisse* (London 1973) page 258.

13. K. Marx and F. Engels, *Manifesto of the Communist Party* (Moscow, no date) page 73.

14. Marx, *Capital* volume 1, pages 592–95.

15. Marx, *Capital* volume 1, page 592.

16. Marx, *Grundrisse*, page 414.

17. See Marx, *Capital* volume 1, chapter 25.

18. Marx, *Capital* volume 1, pages 626–27.

19. Marx, *Capital* volume 3 (Moscow 1962) page 429.

20. Marx, *Capital* volume 3, pages 428–29.

21. Engels, 'Critique of the Erfurt Programme,' in Marx and Engels, *Werke* (Berlin 1963) volume 22, pages 231–22 (Engels' emphasis).

22. For the sources of this information, see Peter Binns and Mike Haynes, 'New Theories of Eastern European Class Societies,' in *International Socialism*, second series, number 7 (Winter 1980) page 34.

23. Lenin not only wrote the preface to Bukharin's major book, *Imperialism and World Economy*, but was recommending it as the major text on the subject as late as 1921.

24. Quoted in Peter Binns, 'Understanding the New Cold War,' in *International Socialism*, second series, number 19 (Spring 1983) pages 6–7.

25. Cliff, *State Capitalism in Russia*, page 203.

26. N Bukharin, *Imperialism and World Economy* (London 1972) page 157, note.

27. V Lenin, *Collected Works*, third Russian edition, volume 25, pages 473–4, quoted in Cliff, *State Capitalism in Russia*, pages 144–5.

28. Quoted in Trotsky, *The Third International After Lenin* (New York 1936) page 13.

29. Quoted in Trotsky, *The Third International After Lenin*, page 46.

30. Quoted in Deutscher, page 232.

31. Cliff, *State Capitalism in Russia*, page 39.

32. See Cliff, *A Socialist Review* (London 1966) pages 116–17.

33. Cliff, *State Capitalism in Russia*, page 46.

34. S Cohn, *Economic Development in the Soviet Union* (Lexington, Massachusetts 1970) page 71.

35. H Schwartz, *The Soviet Economy since Stalin* (London 1965) pages 45–6.

36. Marx, *Capital* volume 1, pages 186–7.

37. Marx, *Grundrisse*, page 513 (emphasis in original).

38. Marx, *Grundrisse*, page 224 (emphasis in original).

39. Marx, *Capital* volume 1, page 41.

40. Sources: Chris Harman, *Bureaucracy and Revolution in Eastern Europe* (London 1974) page 255; A Grossman, writing in *Problems of Communism*, March 1976; and A Zauberman, writing in *Problems of Communism*, March/April 1978, page 56.

41. Harman, 'Poland: The Crisis of State Capitalism,' in *International Socialism*, first series, number 93.

42. Colin Barker and Kara Weber, *Solidarność—From Gdansk to Military Repression* (London 1982) page 140.

43.   See Grossman, in *Problems of Communism*.

44.   Harman, *Bureaucracy and Revolution in Eastern Europe*, page 256.

APPENDIX 1: EIGHTY YEARS SINCE THE RUSSIAN REVOLUTION

1   V. I. Lenin, *Collected Works*, Volume 28 (Progress Publishers, Moscow, 1977), pp. 292–93.

2   Quoted in John Rees, "In Defense of October," in *International Socialism* 52, Autumn 1991, London, p. 9.

3   Ibid.

4   Philip Foner, editor, *The Bolshevik Revolution: Its Impact on American Radicals, Liberals and Labor* (International Publishers, New York, 1967), p. 20.

5   For those interested in pursuing any particular aspect of the Russian Revolution see the suggested reading list for a good start.

6   Isaac Deutscher writes in *The Prophet Outcast:* "For two hours, speaking in German, he addressed an audience of about 2,000 people. His theme was the Russian Revolution. As the authorities had allowed the lecture on the condition that he would avoid controversy, he spoke in a somewhat professorial manner, giving the audience the quintessence of the three volumes of his just concluded *History*. His restraint did not conceal the depth and force of this conviction; the address was a vindication of the October Revolution, all the more effective because free of apologetics and frankly acknowledging partial failures and mistakes. Nearly twenty-five years later members of the audience still recalled the lecture with vivid appreciation as an oratorical feat." Isaac Deutscher, *The Prophet Outcast, Trotsky: 1929–1940* (Oxford University Press, London, 1970), pp.184–85.

7   Marcel Liebman, *The Russian Revolution* (Jonathan Cape, London, 1970), p. 17n50.

8   Ibid., p. 24.

9   Ibid., p. 19.

10   Dominic Lieven, "Russia, Europe and World War I," in Edward Acton, Vladimir Iu. Cherniaev, William Rosenberg, eds., *Critical Companion to the Russian Revolution, 1914–1921* (Indiana University Press, Bloomington and Indianapolis, 1997), p. 37.

11   Leon Trotsky, *Stalin* (Grosset and Dunlap, New York, 1941), p. 422.

12   Leon Trotsky, *History of the Russian Revolution* (Pluto Press, London, 1997), p. 31. Hereafter referred to as *HRR*.

13   S. A. Smith, *Red Petrograd: Revolution in the Factories 1917–1918* (Cambridge University Press, New York, 1983), pp. 9–10.

14   One dessiatine equals 2.7 acres.

15   *Leon Trotsky Speaks*, pp. 252–255.

16   *HRR*, p. 19.

17   Neil Harding, ed, *Marxism in Russia: Key Documents 1879–1906* (Cambridge University Press, 1983), p. 16.

18 Paul Le Blanc, *Lenin and the Revolutionary Party* (Humanities Press International Inc.: Atlantic Highlands, NJ, 1990), pp. 17–18.

19 Ibid., p. 18.

20 Ibid.

21 Ibid., pp. 45–46.

22 Ibid., pp. 66–67.

23 Neil Harding, *op. cit.*, p. 224.

24 Paul Frölich, *Rosa Luxemburg* (Pluto Press, London, 1970), p. 89.

25 V. I. Lenin, "Two Tactics of Social-Democracy in the Democratic Revolution," in *Collected Works*, Volume 9 (Progress Publishers, Moscow, 1977), p. 57.

26 Quoted in Cliff, *Lenin*, Volume 1, p. 143.

27 V. I. Lenin, Volume 9, op. cit., pp. 56–57.

28 Duncan Hallas, *Trotsky's Marxism* (Pluto Press, London, 1978), p. 15.

29 Ibid.

30 Ibid.

31 *Leon Trotsky Speaks*, Ed. by Sarah Novell (Pathfinder Press, New York, 1972) p. 256.

32 Leon Trotsky, *1905* (Pelican Books, Middlesex, England, 1973), p. 122.

33 Ibid., pp. 238–239.

34 Leon Trotsky, *My Life* (Penguin Books, Ltd., Middlesex, England, 1974), p. 180.

35 Ernest Mandel, "Rosa Luxemburg and German Social Democracy," in *Revolutionary Marxism and Social Reality in the 20th Century* (Humanities Press International Inc.: Atlantic Highlands, NJ, 1994), pp. 37–38.

36 Julius Braunthal, *History of the International, 1864–1914* (Frederick A. Praeger, Inc. Publishers, New York, 1967), p. 298.

37 Neil Harding, *Lenin's Political Thought* (Humanities Press International Inc.: Atlantic Highlands, NJ, 1983), p. 249.

38 David Mandel, "Intelligentsia and the Working Class in 1917," *Critique* 14, 1981, London, pp. 69–70.

39 Lewis H. Siegelbaum, *The Politics of Industrial Mobilization in Russia, 1914–1917* (The Macmillan Press, Ltd., London, 1983), p. 18.

40 Quoted in Olga Hess Gankin and H. H. Fisher, *The Bolsheviks and the World War: The Origin of the Third International* (Stanford University Press, Stanford, Calif., 1976), p. 59.

41 Leon Trotsky, *My Life* (Penguin Books, Harmondsworth, Middlesex, 1975), p. 257.

42 Trotsky, *HRR*, p. 42.

43 Tony Cliff, *Lenin: All Power to the Soviets*, Volume 2 (Pluto Press, London, 1976), p.64.

44 Alexander Shlyapnikov, *On the Eve of 1917: Reminiscences from the Revolutionary Underground* (Allison & Busby, London, 1982), p. 224.

45 Paul Dukes, *October and the World: Perspectives on the Russian Revolution* (Macmillan Press, London, 1979), p. 85.

46 Leon Trotsky, *1905*, op. cit., p. 91.

47 Quoted in Tony Cliff, *Lenin*, Volume 2, op. cit., p. 62.

48 Trotsky, *HRR*, p. 121.

49 Ibid.

50 Marcel Liebman, *Leninism Under Lenin* (Jonathan Cape, Ltd., London, 1975), pp. 117-118. The Bolshevik Party did not issue its first leaflet until February 27. Sukhanov notes that the Bolshevik Party leaders present at the start of the February Revolution were unsure of themselves. He describes a meeting on February 25th at which their "flatfootedness or, more properly, their incapacity to think their way into the political problem and formulate it, had a depressing effect on us." Quoted in Liebman, op. cit., p. 117.

51 Trotsky, *HRR*, p. 102.

52 Ibid., p. 123.

53 Lionel Kochan, *Russia in Revolution* (Weidenfeld & Nicolson, London, 1966) p. 186.

54 Ibid., p. 187.

55 Ibid.

56 Ibid.

57 Ibid.

58 Ibid., p. 188.

59 Ibid., p. 189.

60 Liebman, *Leninism*, op. cit., p. 121.

61 Kochan, op. cit., p. 212.

62 Ibid.

63 Cliff, *Lenin*, Volume 2, p. 94.

64 Lenin, op. cit., 1p. 104.

65 Kochan, op. cit., p. 207.

66 Quoted in Cliff, Volume 2, pp. 119–120.

67 Quoted in Cliff, Volume 2, p. 121.

68 Liebman, *Leninism*, op. cit., p. 129.

69 Ibid., p. 131.

70 Ibid., p. 130.

71 Quoted in Le Blanc, op. cit., p. 252

72 Lenin, *Collected Works*, Volume 24 (Progress Publishers, Moscow, 1977), pp. 22-23.

73 Liebman, *Leninism*, op. cit., p. 132.

74 *HRR*, p. 337.

75 Kochan, op. cit., p. 223.

76 Ibid., pp. 229–230. The total number of deserters reached more than 2 million by October 1917.

77 Ibid., p. 235.

78 Liebman, *Leninism*, op. cit., p. 158.

79 Duncan Hallas, "All Power to the Soviets," in *International Socialism* 90, July/August, 1976, London, p. 19.

80   Quoted in Tony Cliff, *Lenin*, Volume 2, pp. 290–291.

81   Ibid., p. 298.

82   Ibid., p. 299.

83   Ibid.

84   Ibid., p. 304.

85   *HRR*, p. 17.

86   Liebman, op. cit., p. 201.

87   Marc Ferro, *October 1917* (Routledge & Kegan Paul, London, 1980), p. 2.

88   N.K. Krupskaya, *Reminiscences of Lenin* (International Publishers, New York 1979), pp. 351–352.

89   John Reed, *Ten Days that Shook the World*, p. 14–15.

90   Cliff, *Lenin*, Volume 2, p. 339.

91   Tony Cliff, *Lenin: Revolution Besieged*, Volume 3 (Pluto Press, London, 1978), pp.1–2.

92   Quoted in Le Blanc, op. cit., p. 282.

93   Trotsky, *My Life*, op.cit., pp. 338–339.

94   Ibid., pp. 351–352.

95   Liebman, op. cit., p. 197.

96   Trotsky, *My Life*, op. cit., pp. 348–349.

97   Rosa Luxemburg, "The Russian Revolution," *Rosa Luxemburg Speaks* (Pathfinder Press, New York, 1980), pp. 394–395.

APPENDIX 2: *THE FALL OF STALINISM: TEN YEARS ON*

1   Roger Cohen, "Verdict in Berlin Wall Deaths Is Upheld," *New York Times*, November 9, 1999: p. A10.

2   Thomas L. Friedman, "The War Over Peace," *New York Times*, October 27, 1999: p. A31.

3   George Bush, "Toward a New World Order," *US Department of State Dispatch* 1:3, September 17, 1990: pp. 91–94.

4   Francis Fukuyama, *The End of History and the Last Man* (New York: Free Press, 1992), pp. 108, xi, 89. See also Francis Fukuyama, "The End of History?" *The National Interest* 16, Summer 1989: pp. 3–18, and "Reply to My Critics," *The National Interest* 18, Winter 1989–90: pp. 21–28.

5   Orlando Figes, *A People's Tragedy: The Russian Revolution: 1891–1924* (New York: Penguin Books, 1997), p. 823. Eric Hobsbawm praised Figes' book, asserting that "*A People's Tragedy* will do more to help us understand the Russian Revolution than any book I know" (back cover).

6   See Roger Cohen, "The Accommodations of Adam Michnik," *New York Times Magazine*, November 7, 1999: p. 6:72.

7   Eric Hobsbawm, "Waking from History's Great Dream," interview with Paul Barker, *Independent on Sunday*, February 4, 1990: pp. 3–5, quoted in Tony Cliff, *State Capitalism in Russia*, third edition (Chicago: Bookmarks, 1996), p. x. See also Alex Callinicos, *The Revenge of History: Marxism and the East European Revolutions* (University Park: Pennsylvania State University Press, 1991), p. 12.

8   Hobsbawm, "Waking from History's Great Dream," pp. 3–5. Eric Hobsbawm, "Out of the Ashes," *After the Fall: The Failure of Communism and the Future of Socialism*, Robin Blackburn ed. (New York: Verso, 1991), p. 322. In his preface to the volume, Robin Blackburn, the editor of *New Left Review*, similarly argues that "the Left must respect the complex structures of self-determination which the market embodies" (xiv).

9   Hobsbawm, "Out of the Ashes," p. 323.

10 Alexander Cockburn, *The Golden Age Is in Us: Journeys and Encounters, 1987–1994* (New York: Verso, 1995), p. 226.

11 Karl Marx and Frederick Engels, *The Communist Manifesto*, Samuel Moore trans. (New York: Penguin Classics, 1967), p. 92.

12 Ibid., p. 104.

13 Ibid., p. 105.

14 Engels, "Preface to the English Edition of 1888," in Marx and Engels, *Communist Manifesto*, p. 62. See also Hal Draper, "The Principle of Self-Emancipation in Marx and Engels," *Socialism from Below*, Ernest Haberkern, ed. (Atlantic Highlands, New Jersey: Humanities Press, 1992), pp. 243–71.

15 V. I. Lenin, *The State and Revolution*, Robert Service, trans. (New York: Penguin Classics, 1992), p. 26. Lenin here is paraphrasing Marx's *The Eighteenth Brumaire of Louis Bonaparte* (New York: International Publishers, 1963), p. 122.

16 Moshe Lewin, *Lenin's Last Struggle*, A.M. Sheridan-Smith, trans. (London: Pluto Press, 1975), p. 3. See also John Rees, "In Defence of October," in Rees et al., *In Defence of October: A Debate on the Russian Revolution* (Chicago: Bookmarks, 1997), p. 12, and Leon Trotsky, *The History of the Russian Revolution*, Max Eastman trans. (London: Pluto Press, 1997), pp. 1233–37.

17 Victor Serge, *Year One of the Russian Revolution*, Peter Sedgwick trans. (New York: Writers and Readers, 1992), p. 328.

18 See Chris Harman, *The Lost Revolution: Germany 1918–23*, second edition (Chicago: Bookmarks, 1997).

19 See David S. Foglesong, *America's Secret War Against Bolshevism: U.S. Intervention in the Russian Civil War, 1917–1920* (Chapel Hill: University of North Carolina Press, 1995).

20 Michael Reiman, *The Birth of Stalinism: The USSR on the Eve of the "Second Revolution,"* George Saunders, trans. (Bloomington: Indiana University Press, 1987), p. 2.

21 Tony Cliff, *Trotsky: The Sword of the Revolution, 1917–1923* (Chicago: Bookmarks, 1990), p. 159.

22 Ibid.

23 Victor Serge, *Revolution in Danger: Writings From Russia, 1919/1920*, Ian Birchall, trans. (London: Redwords, 1997), p. 5.

24 Tony Cliff, *The Revolution Besieged: Lenin 1912–1923* (Chicago: Bookmarks, 1987), p. 204.

25 See Trotsky's *History of the Russian Revolution*, Appendix II, "Socialism in a Separate Country?" pp. 1219–57, and Leon Trotsky, *The Revolution Betrayed:*

What Is the Soviet Union and Where Is it Going? Max Eastman, trans. (New York: Pathfinder, 1972), pp. 32, 291–308.

26   Karl Marx, *Capital: A Critique of Political Economy*, vol. 1, Ben Fowkes, trans. (New York: Penguin Classics, 1990), p. 775, pp. 871–940.

27   G.K. Ordzhonikidze quoted in Cliff, *State Capitalism*, p. 102.

28   Cliff, *State Capitalism*, p. 43.

29   Leon Trotsky, "A Graphic History of Bolshevism," in *Writings of Leon Trotsky [1938-39]* (New York: Pathfinder, 1974), p. 337.

30   Trotsky, "A Graphic History of Bolshevism," pp. 333–34.

31   See Cliff, *State Capitalism*, p. 166.

32   Ibid., p. 182.

33   Marx and Engels, *Communist Manifesto*, p. 104.

34   Trotsky, *History of the Russian Revolution*, p. 17.

35   Serge, *Revolution in Danger*, p. 12. Serge stressed that the Bolsheviks also kept open theaters and centers of learning during this time: "The Red city is suffering and fighting so that one day leisure and art shall be the property of all" (p. 13).

36   Cliff, *State Capitalism*, p. 51.

37   Ibid., p. 60.

38   Ibid., p. 42.

39   Ibid., pp. 55, 59.

40   Marx and Engels, *Communist Manifesto*, p. 97.

41   For an analysis of the transformation of the Communist Parties into tools of Russian foreign policy, see Duncan Hallas' *The Comintern* (London: Bookmarks, 1985).

42   Cliff, *Russia: A Marxist Analysis*, third edition (London: Pluto Press, 1970), p. 333.

43   On Germany, see Donny Gluckstein, *The Nazis, Capitalism and the Working Class* (Chicago: Bookmarks, 1999) and Daniel Guérin, *The Brown Plague: Travels in Late Weimar and Early Nazi Germany*, Robert Schwartzwald trans. (Durham, NC: Duke University Press, 1994).

44   See Gabriel Kolko, *The Politics of War: The World and United States Foreign Policy, 1943-1945* (New York: Vintage, 1968), pp. 144–45.

45   Ygael Gluckstein [Tony Cliff], *Stalin's Satellites in Europe* (Boston: Beacon Press, 1952), p. 229.

46   Frederick Engels, *Anti-Dühring: Herr Eugen Dühring's Revolution in Science* (Peking: Foreign Languages Press, 1976), p. 359. See Hal Draper, *Karl Marx's Theory of Revolution, Volume IV: Critique of Other Socialisms* (New York: Monthly Review Press, 1990), pp. 41–106, for an elaboration of this argument.

47   See Alan M. Wald, *The New York Intellectuals: The Rise and Decline of the Anti-Stalinist Left from the 1930s to the 1980s* (Chapel Hill: University of North Carolina Press, 1987).

48   Tony Cliff, *Stalinist Russia: A Marxist Analysis* (London: Michael Kidron, 1955), pp. 227-28. Compare with Cliff, *State Capitalism*, pp. 271–72.

49   On these conflicts, see Chris Harman, *Class Struggles in Eastern Europe 1945–83*, third edition (Chicago: Bookmarks, 1988).

50   Tony Cliff, "Balance of Powerlessness," *Socialist Review* 145, September 1991: p. 10.

51   Zoltan Bassa, "Hungary," *Socialist Review* 235, November 1999: p. 20.

52   Harman, "The Storm Breaks," pp. 13–18.

53   Gabi Engelhardt, "Germany," *Socialist Review* 235, November 1999: p. 17.

54   See Roger Cohen, "Haphazardly, Berlin Wall Fell a Decade Ago," *New York Times*, November 9, 1999: pp. A1, A10.

55   John Tagliabue, reporting for the *New York Times*, November 20, 1989, in *The Collapse of Communism*, third edition, Bernard Gwertzman and Michael T. Kaufman eds. (New York: Times Books, 1991), pp. 229–31.

56   See Esther B. Fein's report in *The Collapse of Communism*, pp. 240–42.

57   See Steven Greenhouse's report in *The Collapse of Communism*, pp. 237–39.

58   Engelhardt, "Germany," p. 17.

59   For an instructive comparison, see Mike Haynes, "Class and Crisis: The Transition in Eastern Europe," *International Socialism* 54, Spring 1992: pp. 45–104, especially pp. 58–69.

60   Elemer Hankiss quoted in Haynes, p. 53.

61   Andy Zebrowski, note to Philip Ilkowski, "Poland," *Socialist Review* 235, November 1999: p. 18.

62   Chubais quoted in Anthony Robinson, "Barriers Between Ins and Outs," *Financial Times*, October 2, 1998, World Economy and Finance Survey section: p. xxvi.

63   Roger Cohen, "Poland's Glossy Capitalism Displays a Darker Underside," *New York Times*, September 30, 1999: p. A8.

64   "Ten Years Since the Wall Fell," *The Economist* 353/8144, November 6, 1999: p. 22.

65   "Worth Living? Life Expectancy, 1987-1997," Table, *The Economist* 353/8144, November 6, 1999: p. 23.

66   Paul Lewis, "Aid to Poor Could Miss Targets And Stall, World Bank Reports," *New York Times*, April 27, 1999: p. A6.

67   Michael Specter, "Dr. Dostoyevsky's Diagnosis; Deep in the Russian Soul, a Lethal Darkness," *New York Times*, June 8, 1997: p. 4:1.

68   Michael Specter, "The Most Tainted Place On Earth," *New York Times Magazine*, February 8, 1998: p. 6:49.

69   See United Nations Development Program, *Human Development Report 1999* (New York: Oxford University Press, 1999). For a useful summary of the key findings, see Bill Roberts, "Briefing: Human Underdevelopment Report," *International Socialist Review* 6, Spring 1999: p. 42.

70   Michael Holman, "Bowed by a Crippling Burden," *Financial Times*, October 2, 1998, World Economy and Finance Survey section: p. xxii.

71   Paul Berman, "Ten Years After 1989," *Dissent*, Fall 1999: p. 9.

72   Adam Michnik, "Ten Years After 1989," *Dissent*, Fall 1999: pp. 14–15.

73   Marx, *Eighteenth Brumaire*, p. 15.

74   Harman, *Class Struggles in Eastern Europe*, p. 1.

75   Daniel Singer, *Whose Millennium? Theirs or Ours?* (New York: Monthly Review Press, 1999), p. 279.

76   See, for example, Howard Zinn, *Marx in Soho: A Play on History* (Cambridge: South End Press, 1999) for one excellent attempt at such reclamation. See also Singer's *Whose Millennium?* On socialism from below, see also Hal Draper, *Socialism from Below*, especially "The Two Souls of Socialism" (pp. 2–33).

ABOUT HAYMARKET BOOKS

Haymarket Books is a radical, independent, nonprofit book publisher based in Chicago.

Our mission is to publish books, particularly new and classical works of Marxism, that contribute to struggles for social and economic justice. We strive to make our books a vibrant and organic part of social movements and the education and development of a critical, engaged, international left.

We take inspiration and courage from our namesakes, the Haymarket martyrs, who gave their lives fighting for a better world. Their 1886 struggle for the eight-hour day—which gave us May Day, the international workers' holiday—reminds workers around the world that ordinary people can organize and struggle for their own liberation. These struggles continue today across the globe—struggles against oppression, exploitation, poverty, and war.

Since our founding in 2001, Haymarket Books has published more than five hundred titles. Radically independent, we seek to drive a wedge into the risk-averse world of corporate book publishing. Our authors include Eqbal Ahmad, Arundhati Roy, Angela Y. Davis, Howard Zinn, Ian Birchall, Ahmed Shawki, Paul Le Blanc, Mike Davis, Kim Scipes, Ilan Pappé, Michael Roberts, Sharon Smith, Dave Zirin, Keeanga-Yamahtta Taylor, Nick Turse, Kim Moody, Danny Katch, Jeffery R. Webber, Paul D'Amato, Amira Hass, Sherry Wolf, Naomi Klein, and Neil Davidson. We are also the trade publishers of the acclaimed Historical Materialism Book Series, and of the Studies in Critical Social Sciences book series, as well as Dispatch Books.

Shop our full catalog online at www.haymarketbooks.org.